BERNIE

BERNIE

TED RALL

NEW YORK / OAKLAND

ACKNOWLEDGMENTS

Michael Briggs, Sandy Dijkstra, Jon Gilbert, Lauren Hooker, Bonnie D. Miller, Bill Press, Carol Press, Dan Simon

■   ■   ■

A Seven Stories Press First Edition

Seven Stories Press
140 Watts Street
New York, NY 10013
www.sevenstories.com

Library of Congress Cataloging-in-Publication Data

Names: Rall, Ted.
Title: Bernie / by Ted Rall.
Description: First edition. | New York : Seven Stories Press, 2016.
Identifiers: LCCN 2015046626| ISBN 9781609806989 (paperback) | ISBN 9781609806996 (e-book)
Subjects: LCSH: Sanders, Bernard. | Sanders, Bernard--Political and social views. | Sanders, Bernard--Comic books, strips, etc. | Legislators--United States--Biography. | Presidential candidates--United States--Biography. | Socialists--United States--Biography. | United States. Congress. Senate--Biography. | BISAC: COMICS & GRAPHIC NOVELS / Nonfiction. | BIOGRAPHY & AUTOBIOGRAPHY / Political. | POLITICAL SCIENCE / Political Process / Elections.
Classification: LCC E840.8.S26 R35 2016 | DDC 328.73/092--dc23
LC record available at http://lccn.loc.gov/2015046626

Printed in the USA.

9 8 7 6 5 4 3 2 1

BERNIE

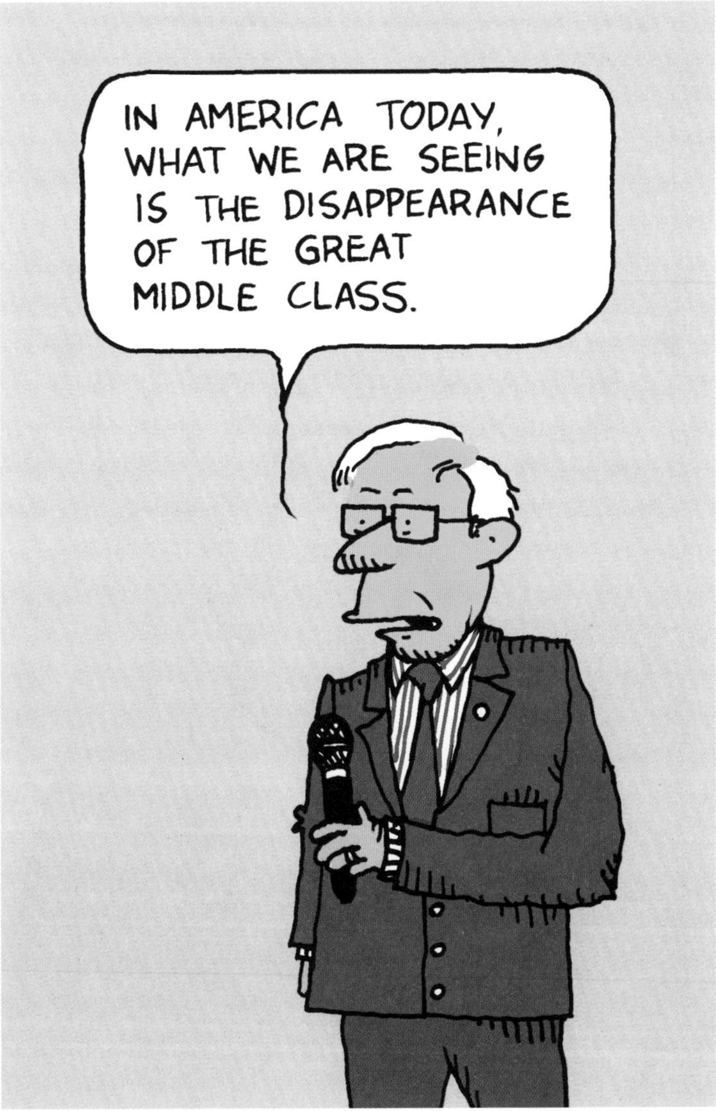
IN AMERICA TODAY, WHAT WE ARE SEEING IS THE DISAPPEARANCE OF THE GREAT MIDDLE CLASS.

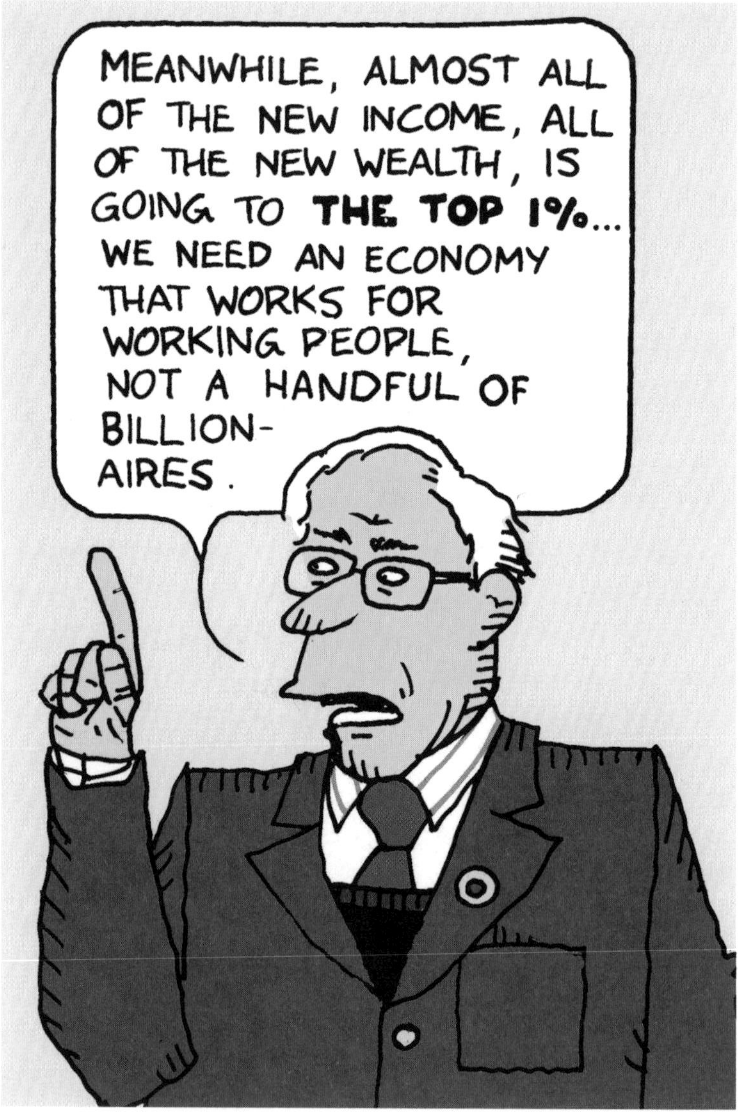
MEANWHILE, ALMOST ALL OF THE NEW INCOME, ALL OF THE NEW WEALTH, IS GOING TO **THE TOP 1%**... WE NEED AN ECONOMY THAT WORKS FOR WORKING PEOPLE, NOT A HANDFUL OF BILLION-AIRES.

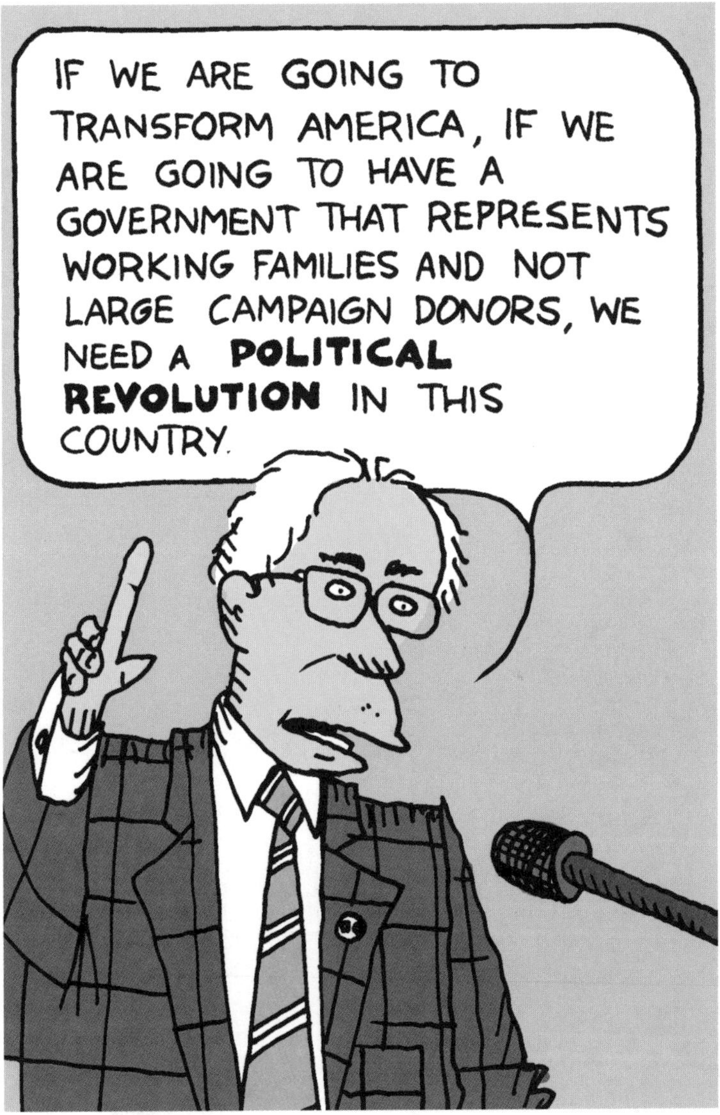
IF WE ARE GOING TO TRANSFORM AMERICA, IF WE ARE GOING TO HAVE A GOVERNMENT THAT REPRESENTS WORKING FAMILIES AND NOT LARGE CAMPAIGN DONORS, WE NEED A POLITICAL REVOLUTION IN THIS COUNTRY.

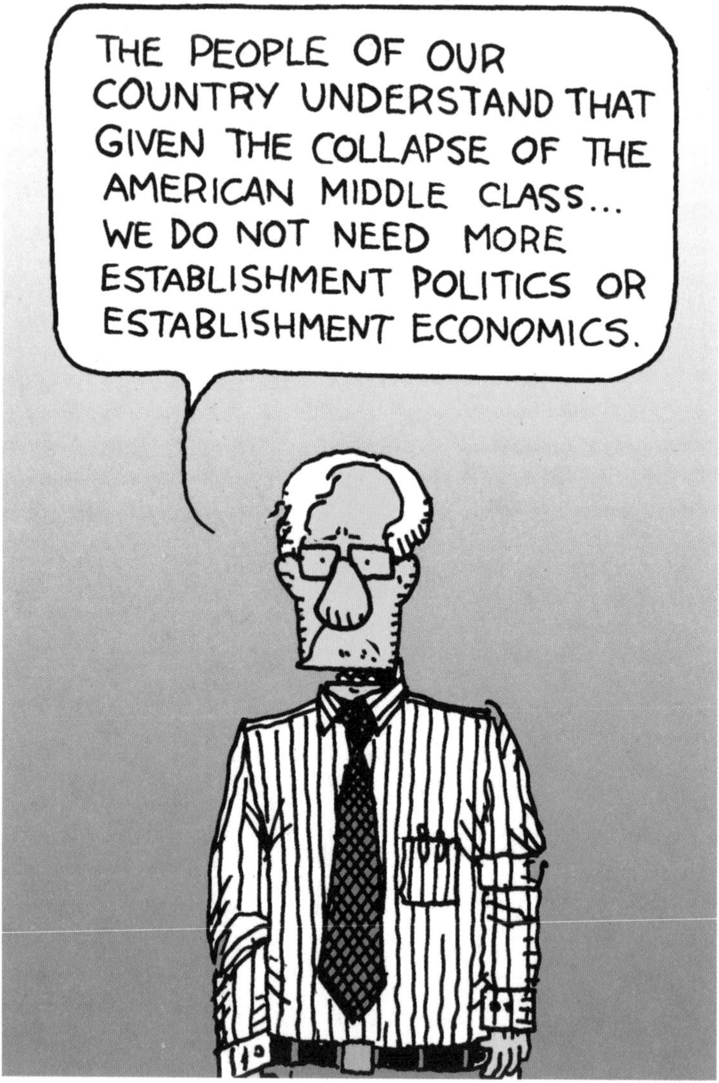
THE PEOPLE OF OUR COUNTRY UNDERSTAND THAT GIVEN THE COLLAPSE OF THE AMERICAN MIDDLE CLASS... WE DO NOT NEED MORE ESTABLISHMENT POLITICS OR ESTABLISHMENT ECONOMICS.

FIRST
THEY
CAME
FOR
THE
LIBERALS

TO UNDERSTAND THE
BERNIE SANDERS
PHENOMENON, LET'S
TAKE A WALK DOWN
DEMOCRATIC PARTY
MEMORY LANE...

1972: DEMOCRATIC PRESIDENTIAL NOMINEE GEORGE McGOVERN LOSES TO INCUMBENT PRESIDENT RICHARD NIXON. IT'S THE BIGGEST LANDSLIDE IN AMERICAN ELECTORAL HISTORY.

McGOVERN IS A WORLD WAR II HERO. IT MAKES NO DIFFERENCE. BECAUSE HE'S LIBERAL, REPUBLICANS SMEAR HIM AS A "COMMUNIST."

1973: DEMOCRATIC PARTY LEADERS CONDUCT AN ELECTION POSTMORTEM. THEY'RE DETERMINED NOT TO REPEAT THE MISTAKES THAT COST THEM 49 OUT OF 50 STATES.

THE EAGLETON THING DIDN'T HELP.

BUT OUR GUY WAS A **HERO**. WE SHOULD NEVER HAVE LOST **THIS BAD**.

VIETNAM DIDN'T EVEN SLOW NIXON DOWN!

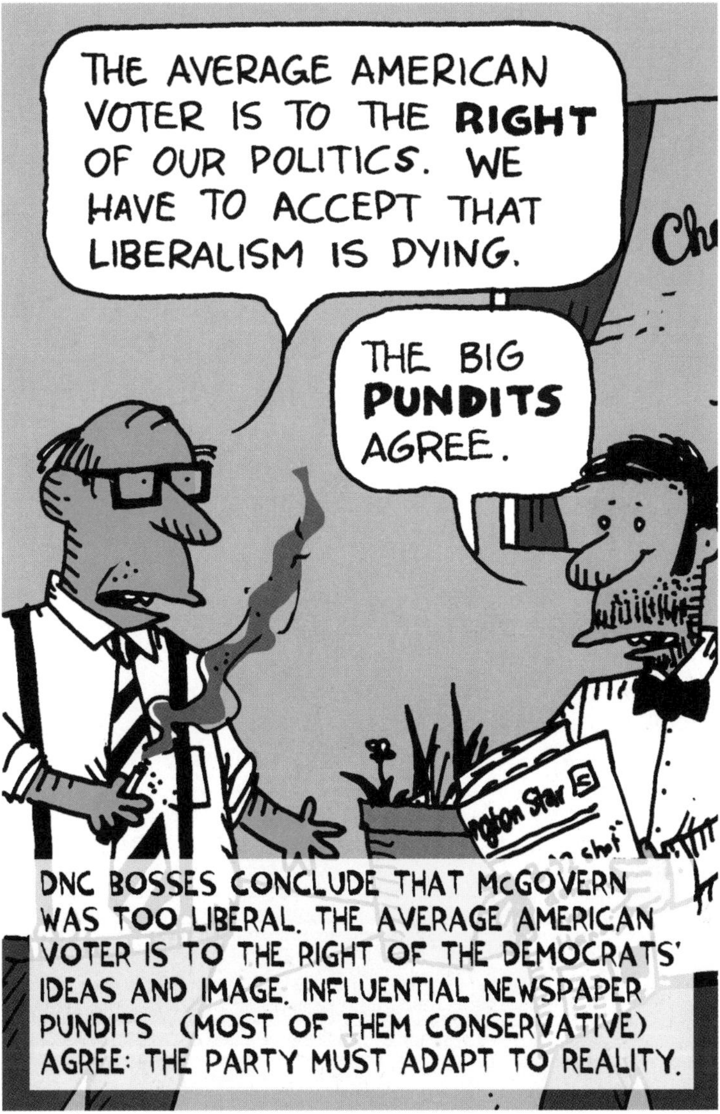
THE AVERAGE AMERICAN VOTER IS TO THE **RIGHT** OF OUR POLITICS. WE HAVE TO ACCEPT THAT LIBERALISM IS DYING.
THE BIG **PUNDITS** AGREE.
DNC BOSSES CONCLUDE THAT McGOVERN WAS TOO LIBERAL. THE AVERAGE AMERICAN VOTER IS TO THE RIGHT OF THE DEMOCRATS' IDEAS AND IMAGE. INFLUENTIAL NEWSPAPER PUNDITS (MOST OF THEM CONSERVATIVE) AGREE: THE PARTY MUST ADAPT TO REALITY.

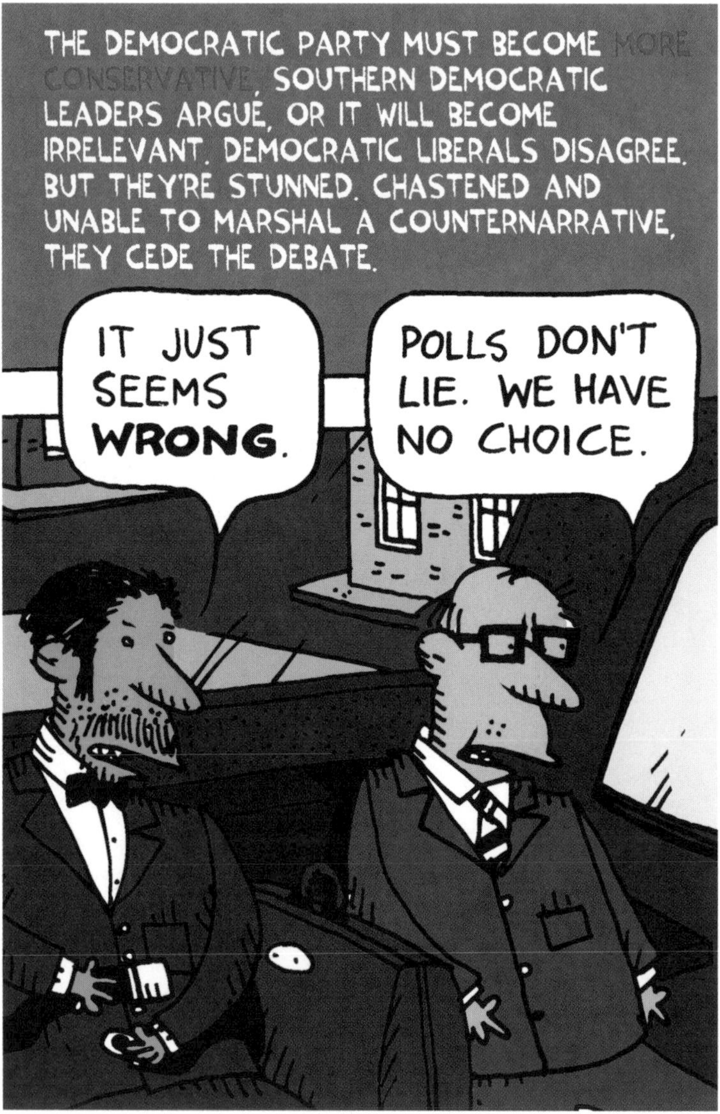
THE DEMOCRATIC PARTY MUST BECOME MORE CONSERVATIVE, SOUTHERN DEMOCRATIC LEADERS ARGUE, OR IT WILL BECOME IRRELEVANT. DEMOCRATIC LIBERALS DISAGREE. BUT THEY'RE STUNNED, CHASTENED AND UNABLE TO MARSHAL A COUNTERNARRATIVE, THEY CEDE THE DEBATE.
IT JUST SEEMS **WRONG**.
POLLS DON'T LIE. WE HAVE NO CHOICE.

THE CENTRISTS SEIZE THE INITIATIVE.
CONSERVATIVE DEMOCRATIC SENATORS
"SCOOP" JACKSON, SAM NUNN, AND
CHARLES ROBB FOUND THE COALITION
FOR A DEMOCRATIC MAJORITY.

Pro-defense

Pro-Vietnam War

Henry "Scoop" Jackson
D-WA

Anti-gay

Sam Nunn
D-GA

Pro-Gulf War

Supported Clarence Thomas

Chuck Robb
D-VA

THE CDM'S MISSION: MOVE THE DEMOCRATS
TO THE RIGHT.

THE "NEW LEFT" HAD BECOME AN
IMPORTANT VOICE WITHIN THE PARTY IN THE
'60s AND EARLY '70s.

THEY MUST BE PURGED, CDMers SAY.
LIBERALS, PROGRESSIVES, SOCIALISTS, AND
OTHER LEFTISTS WILL NO LONGER BE
ALLOWED TO INFLUENCE THE PARTY'S
PLATFORM OR MARKETING.

1976: PRESIDENTIAL CANDIDATE JIMMY CARTER ISN'T A CDM MAN.

AFTER HE NARROWLY DEFEATS INCUMBENT GERALD FORD, CARTER IGNORES CDM SUGGESTIONS FOR CABINET APPOINTMENTS.

YET CARTER IS A CANNY, INTUITIVE POLITICIAN. SENSING OPPORTUNITY, HE YIELDS TO PRESSURE TO PIVOT RIGHT.

MOREOVER, AS A RURAL GEORGIAN, HE ISN'T HARDWIRED FOR STRIDENT LIBERALISM.

IT ISN'T WIDELY RECOGNIZED AT THE TIME --
INDEED, FEW HISTORIANS ACKNOWLEDGE IT
TODAY -- BUT JIMMY CARTER'S ONE-TERM
PRESIDENCY MARKS A TURNING POINT IN
THE DEMOCRATIC PARTY'S SHIFT TO THE
RIGHT.

THE CHANGE IS STRUCTURAL.

"OVER THE YEARS, IN THE
1970s, THE DEMOCRATIC
PARTY BECAME MORE
DEPENDENT
ON
CORPORATE
MONEY. IF
YOU NEED   Bernie
MONEY, YOU   Sanders
GO TO
WEALTHY
PEOPLE."

FDR

Social Security

1977-1980: CARTER BECOMES THE FIRST DEMOCRAT IN MEMORY NOT TO PROPOSE A MAJOR ANTI-POVERTY PROGRAM. AFTER 1972, THERE WILL NEVER BE ANOTHER OLD-SCHOOL LIBERAL "BIG GOVERNMENT" ATTEMPT TO HELP THE POOR.

TRUMAN

CWA
CCC
WPA
Aid to Dependent Children
"Fair Deal"
Medicaid
Fair Labor Standards Act
Work Study
Medicare
LBJ
Food Stamps
Head Start

"AND THAT MAKES YOU A **MORE CONSERVATIVE PARTY.**"

CARTER'S HAWKISH DIPLOMATIC AND MILITARY POLICIES REFLECT HIS PARTY'S RIGHTWARD SHIFT. SEVEN YEARS AFTER CONGRESS ELIMINATED THE VIETNAM-ERA DRAFT, CARTER BRINGS IT HALF-BACK IN THE FORM OF "DRAFT REGISTRATION" BY THE SELECTIVE SERVICE SYSTEM.

(TODAY, 18-YEAR-OLDS STILL SIGN UP AT THE POST OFFICE.)

1979: MOHAMMAD REZA SHAH PAHLAVI, THE DICTATOR/ AMERICAN PUPPET OVERTHROWN BY IRAN'S ISLAMIC REVOLUTION, NEEDS TREATMENT FOR GALLSTONES.

DETERMINED TO HONOR AMERICA'S COMMITMENT TO ITS ALLY, CARTER IGNORES THE THREATS OF IRANIAN REVOLUTIONARIES, ADMITTING HIM TO A HOSPITAL IN NEW YORK.

NEWS OF THE SHAH'S ENTRY INTO THE U.S. PROMPTS RADICAL STUDENTS TO TAKE OVER THE U.S. EMBASSY IN TEHRAN. EMBASSY PERSONNEL ARE HELD HOSTAGE FOR 444 DAYS.

IRANIAN RADICALS ARE STRENGTHENED. DEMOCRATS APPEAR WEAK ON FOREIGN POLICY, TRADITIONALLY THEIR POLITICAL ACHILLES' HEEL.

CARTER'S POPULARITY ERODES.

DECEMBER 1979: THE SOVIET UNION INVADES AFGHANISTAN. BEHIND THE SCENES, THE RUSSIANS ARE SUCKED IN BY A SCHEME COVERTLY INSTIGATED BY CARTER'S MACHIAVELLIAN NATIONAL SECURITY ADVISOR, ZBIGNIEW BRZEZINSKI. BRZEZINSKI CALLS IT THE "AFGHAN TRAP."

IN A SURPRISINGLY AGGRESSIVE MOVE, CARTER ANNOUNCES THAT THE U.S. WILL BOYCOTT THE 1980 OLYMPIC GAMES IN MOSCOW. EVEN AT THE HEIGHT OF THE COLD WAR DURING THE 1950s, THE REPUBLICANS HADN'T POLITICIZED THE OLYMPICS.

IF ONLY THE OLYMPICS HAD NOT BEEN HELD IN BERLIN IN 1936 THE COURSE OF HISTORY COULD HAVE BEEN DIFFERENT.

WE FACE A SIMILAR PROSPECT NOW.

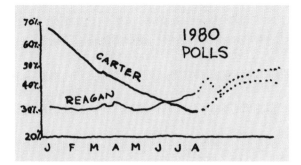

1980 POLLS

OUR CAUSE HAS BEEN, SINCE THE DAYS OF THOMAS JEFFERSON, THE CAUSE OF THE COMMON MAN AND THE COMMON WOMAN.

1980 DEMOCRATIC PRIMARIES: DISMAYED BY CARTER'S ABANDONMENT OF THE PARTY'S HISTORICAL CONCERN FOR THE DOWNTRODDEN AND HIS BELLICOSE ATTITUDE, LIBERALS RALLY AROUND A CHALLENGE TO CARTER BY SENATOR TED KENNEDY, SCION OF THE LEGENDARY POLITICAL FAMILY.

KENNEDY
FOR PRESIDENT

DESPITE CARTER'S SHRINKING SUPPORT -- BY LATE SUMMER 1980, WEAKENED BY THE HOSTAGE CRISIS AND HIGH INFLATION, HIS APPROVAL RATING IS 29% -- PARTY LEADERS PUSH THROUGH LAST-MINUTE CHANGES TO THE RULES GOVERNING CONVENTION DELEGATES' ABILITY TO VOTE THEIR MINDS.

CARTER CRUSHES KENNEDY AND TAKES ON REPUBLICAN RONALD REAGAN.

NOVEMBER 1980: AFFIRMING THE SOON-TO-BE CLICHÉ THAT GIVEN THE CHOICE BETWEEN A FAKE CONSERVATIVE AND A REAL CONSERVATIVE PEOPLE WILL VOTE FOR THE REAL ONE, CARTER LOSES TO RONALD REAGAN IN A HUMILIATINGLY BROAD DEFEAT.

1981: REAGAN, A MOVEMENT CONSERVATIVE VIEWED UNTIL RECENTLY AS AN EXTREMIST, LAUNCHES THE "REAGAN REVOLUTION": SEVERE CUTS TO THE BUDGETS OF SOCIAL AND ANTI-POVERTY PROGRAMS DATING BACK TO FDR'S NEW DEAL.

FOOD BANK

CLOSED

REAGAN BECOMES FAMOUS/INFAMOUS FOR HIS MASSIVE RAMP-UP OF MILITARY SPENDING. BUT IT WASN'T HIS IDEA.

WHAT BECOMES KNOWN AS THE "REAGAN MILITARY BUILDUP" BEGAN WITH CARTER.

TOTAL U.S. MILITARY SPENDING

In billions

Total dollars   Adjusted for inflation

$693.6

$600
500
400
300
200
100
0

1962   1970   1980   1990   2000   2010

Source: WhiteHouse.gov

THE STAR-LEDGER

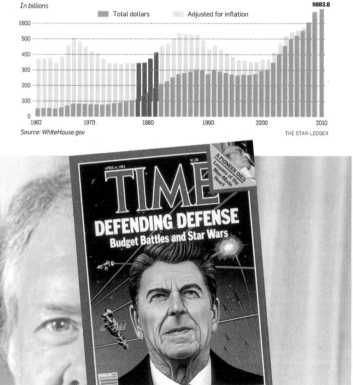

BY THE EARLY 1980s, THE COALITION FOR A DEMOCRATIC MAJORITY IS ON LIFE SUPPORT -- IRONICALLY, BECAUSE IT HAS BEEN SUCCESSFUL. THE LIBERAL AND PROGRESSIVE BASE OF THE DEMOCRATIC PARTY HAS BEEN SO INTERNALLY MARGINALIZED THAT, FOR PRACTICAL PURPOSES, IT NO LONGER EXISTS.

OSTRACIZED BY THE PARTY LEADERSHIP, LEFTIES ARE OUT IN THE POLITICAL WILDERNESS.

1984: AS IF TO PROVE THE "CENTRISTS'" POINT, FORMER VICE PRESIDENT WALTER MONDALE LOSES TO REAGAN -- THIS DESPITE A LONG, DEEP RECESSION MARKED BY HIGH UNEMPLOYMENT.

UNEMPLOYMENT

THOUGH MORE LIBERAL THAN CARTER, MONDALE IS CENTRIST BY HISTORICAL STANDARDS.

33

BOTH PARTIES DRIFT RIGHT. "REAGAN REVOLUTIONARIES" FACE LITTLE OPPOSITION AS THEY DISMANTLE THE NEW DEAL SAFETY NET AND LBJ'S ANTI-POVERTY PROGRAMS.

IF I'M FEELING POOR AND SCARED, I VOTE FOR THE DEMOCRAT.

BUT IF I'M FEELING RESENTFUL AND FLUSH, I VOTE FOR THE REPUBLICAN.

PARTY LEADERS' NEW OBSESSION: "SWING VOTERS" AND "REAGAN DEMOCRATS" — PEOPLE WHO VOTE DEMOCRATIC IN SOME ELECTIONS, REPUBLICAN IN OTHERS.

ACCORDING TO POLITICAL CONSULTANTS, ELECTIONS ARE DECIDED BY THESE INDECISIVE FOLKS.

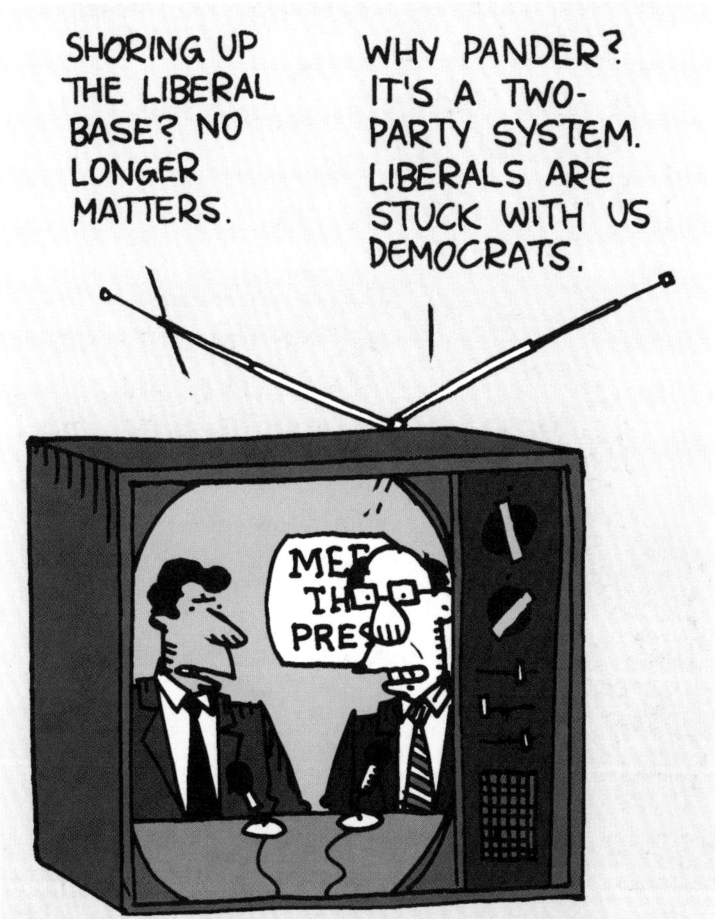
SHORING UP THE LIBERAL BASE? NO LONGER MATTERS.
WHY PANDER? IT'S A TWO-PARTY SYSTEM. LIBERALS ARE STUCK WITH US DEMOCRATS.

LIBERAL CONCERNS -- POVERTY, ENVIRONMENTAL DEGRADATION, RACISM, DISCRIMINATION AGAINST WOMEN, RISING INCOME INEQUALITY -- DISAPPEAR FROM SPEECHES BY DEMOCRATIC CANDIDATES.

THE MEDIA IGNORES THESE ISSUES AS WELL.

TWO-PARTY POLITICS BECOMES A DEBATE BETWEEN CENTER-RIGHT AND RIGHT-RIGHT.

THROUGHOUT THE REAGAN ERA, HOWEVER, THE DEMOCRATIC PARTY TENT STILL INCLUDES A SHRINKING BUT SUBSTANTIAL NUMBER OF DISGRUNTLED LEFTISTS.

THESE ACTIVISTS HOLD DEMONSTRATIONS AGAINST REAGAN'S POLICIES. BUT WITHIN "THEIR" PARTY, THEY'RE IMPOTENT.

CENTER-RIGHT DEMOCRATS CONTINUE TO PRESS THEIR ADVANTAGE. PROMISING TO RECAPTURE "THE VITAL CENTER" OF AMERICAN POLITICS AND EXPEL THE GOP FROM CONGRESS AND THE WHITE HOUSE.

William Gray
D-PA

Tim Wirth
D-CO

Gillis Long
D-LA

Al Gore
D-TN

Dick Gephardt
D-MO

A GROUP OF DEMOCRATIC CONGRESSMEN REVIVES THE OLD CDM IN THE FORM OF THE HOUSE DEMOCRATIC CAUCUS'S "COMMITTEE ON PARTY EFFECTIVENESS."

Al From

DLC

THE ONLY DIFFERENCE BETWEEN THE DEMOCRATIC AND REPUBLICAN PARTIES IS THE VELOCITY WITH WHICH THEIR KNEES HIT THE FLOOR WHEN CORPORATIONS KNOCK.

COALESCING AROUND STRATEGIST AL FROM'S "DEMOCRATIC LEADERSHIP COUNCIL," THIS CENTER-RIGHT GROUP BECOMES KNOWN AS THE "NEW DEMOCRATS," OR "THIRD WAY" DEMOCRATS.

IN DISARRAY AND DEPRESSED, DISPIRITED PROGRESSIVES LIKE RALPH NADER CONSIDER ABANDONING THE PARTY ENTIRELY.

DLC POLICY GOALS: "WELFARE REFORM,"
MARKET-BASED (NOT GOVERNMENT-BASED)
POLICIES, OPPOSITION TO SINGLE-PAYER
HEALTH CARE, SCHOOL VOUCHERS, CHARTER
SCHOOLS, FREE TRADE DEALS LIKE NAFTA,
PARTIAL PRIVATIZATION OF SOCIAL
SECURITY, TAX CUTS FOR THE MIDDLE CLASS.

IDEOLOGICALLY, DLC POLICIES ARE SITUATED
RIGHT OF THE REPUBLICAN PARTY IN 1972.

THE DEMOCRATIC PARTY HAS
AN IMPORTANT CHOICE TO
MAKE: DO WE WANT TO **VENT**
OR DO WE WANT TO **GOVERN**?

Sen.
Evan
Bayh
D-IN

Chmn.,
DLC,
2003

THE DLC QUICKLY BECOMES INFLUENTIAL
AND WELL-FUNDED, DOMINATING
DEMOCRATIC POLICYMAKING WELL INTO
THE ADMINISTRATION OF BARACK OBAMA.

1988: **DEMOCRATS CONTINUE WITH THE DLC'S NEW "MODERATE GOVERNOR" STRATEGY, NOMINATING MICHAEL DUKAKIS FOR PRESIDENT.**

Dukakis riding a tank was the iconic image of the campaign. People thought he was pretending to be a soldier. That made him seem phony.

DUKAKIS LOSES TO REAGAN'S LESS-THAN-THRILLING VICE PRESIDENT, GEORGE H. W. BUSH.

IT'S A ROUT.

THE DLC EXPLOITS THIS LATEST DEFEAT TO PUSH THE PARTY STILL FURTHER RIGHT. TRUE, DUKAKIS WAS A MODERATE. ALSO TRUE, THE DLC ENDORSED HIM. NOW THEY SAY DUKAKIS'S HOME *STATE* OF MASSACHUSETTS HAD TOO LIBERAL OF A REPUTATION NATIONALLY.

"[I WILL] CUT 100,000 BUREAUCRATS AND PUT 100,000 NEW POLICE OFFICERS ON YOUR STREETS OF AMERICAN CITIES." — JULY 16, 1992

"MY PLAN OFFERS $50 BILLION IN... NEW INCENTIVES FOR THE PRIVATE SECTOR."

—JUNE 28, 1992

43

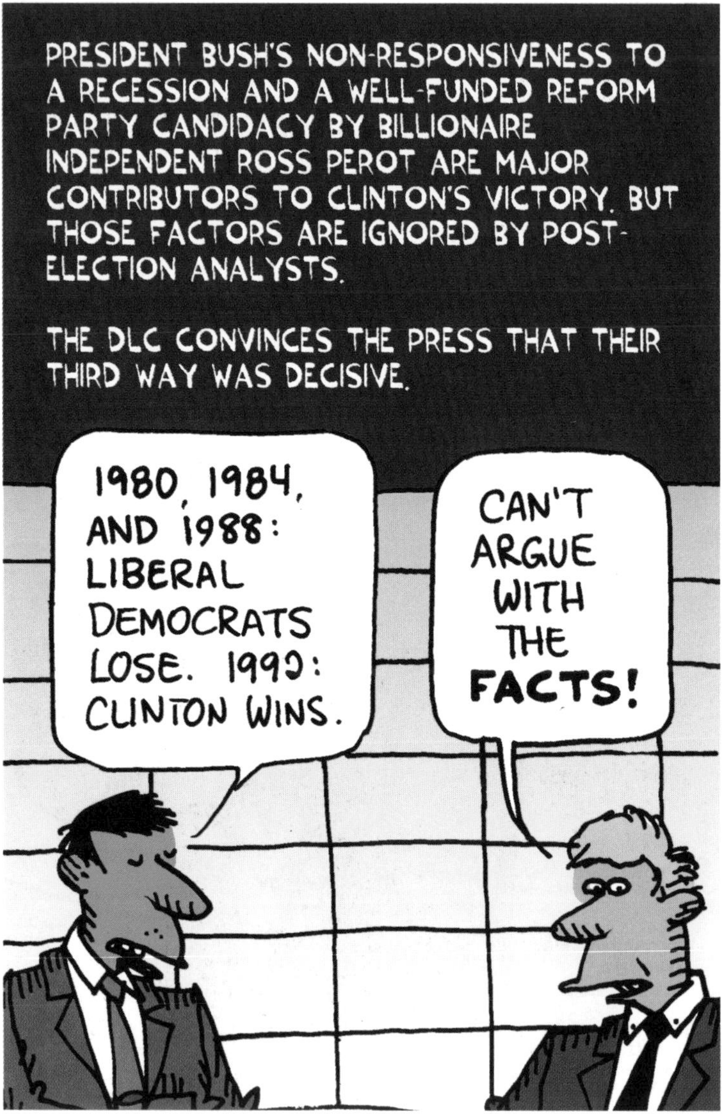
PRESIDENT BUSH'S NON-RESPONSIVENESS TO A RECESSION AND A WELL-FUNDED REFORM PARTY CANDIDACY BY BILLIONAIRE INDEPENDENT ROSS PEROT ARE MAJOR CONTRIBUTORS TO CLINTON'S VICTORY. BUT THOSE FACTORS ARE IGNORED BY POST-ELECTION ANALYSTS.
THE DLC CONVINCES THE PRESS THAT THEIR THIRD WAY WAS DECISIVE.
1980, 1984, AND 1988: LIBERAL DEMOCRATS LOSE. 1992: CLINTON WINS.
CAN'T ARGUE WITH THE FACTS!

BILL CLINTON'S POLLSTER DICK MORRIS EMBODIES THE THIRD WAY. THE BIG-IDEA PROGRAMS OF THE 1960s TURNED VOTERS OFF, MORRIS TELLS THE PRESIDENT. SMALL-BORE WEDGE ISSUES CAN WIN CAMPAIGNS WITHOUT TAKING RISKS.

GAYS IN THE MILITARY! FLAG BURNING! NOW **THOSE** ARE THE ISSUES A DEMOCRAT CAN **WIN!**

MORRIS USES GEOMETRY: "TRIANGULATION" OF THE HARD-CORE POSITIONS OF THE AMERICAN LEFT AND RIGHT MEET SOMEWHERE IN THE MIDDLE (A.K.A. THE "VITAL CENTER").

THE MAN WHO HAS CLINTON'S EAR
Dick Morris

Triangulated
Ideology

Left
Wing

Middle
ground

Right
wing

THIS IS WHERE A CANDIDATE WHO WANTS TO WIN MUST BE. *POLITICIANS SHOULD NOT LEAD THE PEOPLE.*

IN MORRIS'S VIEW, A *PRESIDENT SHOULD FOLLOW* THE VIEWS ALREADY HELD BY THE AVERAGE VOTER.

1990s: LIBERALISM IS ALMOST DEAD.

WITH NO MAINSTREAM POLITICIANS ACTIVELY
PROMOTING THE CAUSE, NO THINK TANKS
CREATING A THEORETICAL FRAMEWORK FOR
THEIR POINT OF VIEW, AND CORPORATE NEWS
MEDIA IN THRALL TO CENTRISM, LEFTIES
SURFACE RARELY...

...AND THEN ONLY TO SALVAGE THE
REMNANTS OF THEIR OLD ACHIEVEMENTS.

POLITICS

Democrats Fight to Restore Curbed Programs

BY JOHN H. CUSHMAN JR.

WASHINGTON, March 13 — Senate Democrats sou!
restore environmental programs that have been
during the long standoff over the budget, as
Clinton Administration vowed again to veto
spending bill that undercut its environment
poll data that shou
blico

NO ONE IN CONGRESS PROPOSES BILLS TO REDUCE POVERTY OR TO IMPROVE PRISON CONDITIONS OR TO ELIMINATE REDLINING. THE COLLAPSE OF THE SOVIET UNION IN 1991 PROMPTS A LITTLE BIT OF TALK ABOUT A "PEACE DIVIDEND" -- TAKING MONEY AWAY FROM COLD WAR-ERA MILITARY SPENDING AND DEDICATING IT TO DOMESTIC NEEDS -- WHICH QUICKLY FADES AWAY UNDER CLINTON.

State of the Union Address, 1993

CAPTURE THE **PEACE DIVIDEND** FOR INVEST- MENT PURPOSES, AND... SWITCH THE BALANCE IN THE BUDGET FROM CONSUMPTION TO **MORE INVESTMENT.**

LIBERALS AND PROGRESSIVES ARE FROZEN OUT. THEIR VIEWS DON'T APPEAR IN THE NATION'S OPINION PAGES OR ON CABLE TV NEWS. THE PRESIDENT DOESN'T HEAR FROM THEM AT CABINET MEETINGS.

REPUBLICAN STRATEGISTS HAVE SUCCESSFULLY FRAMED THE "L WORD" ITSELF -- "LIBERAL" -- AS AN EPITHET.

BILL CLINTON EMERGES FROM HIS TWO TERMS IN OFFICE WITH A LIST OF POLICY ACHIEVEMENTS THAT A REPUBLICAN WOULD BE PROUD OF. CLINTON IS A DINO -- "DEMOCRAT IN NAME ONLY." HE BALANCES THE FEDERAL BUDGET AND REFORMS WELFARE ON THE BACKS OF THE POOR. HE SPENDS HIS POLITICAL CAPITAL ON NAFTA AND THE WTO.

WELFARE REFORM

DEFENSE OF MARRIAGE ACT

BOMBING SOMALIA

DON'T ASK, DON'T TELL

NAFTA

BOMBING AFGHANISTAN

TRADITIONAL DEMOCRATIC ALLIES LIKE BIG LABOR, WEAKENED BY ANTI-UNION LEGISLATION AND DEINDUSTRIALIZATION, WITHER AWAY, NO LONGER ABLE TO GET DEMOCRATS ELECTED.

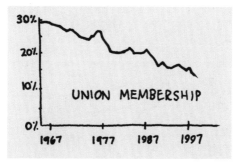

ALIENATED LIBERAL DEMOCRATS VOTE IN LOWER NUMBERS. THE DLC IS STILL CHASING SWING VOTERS.

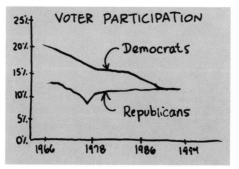

LEFT DEMOCRATS COULD HEAD OUT INTO THE STREETS, BUT MARCHES HAVE BEEN REDUCED TO STREET THEATER, A RELIC OF THE 1960s.

DEMS COMFORT THEMSELVES WITH THE THOUGHT THAT A TWO-TERM DEMOCRAT IN THE WHITE HOUSE IS A VICTORY.

SORT OF.

THE NEW YORK TIMES, DECEMBER 20, 1998

The Face of Eco-Terrorism

BY PODRO PHILLIPS

FUR IS MURDER E.L.F.

Vail Ski Resort Arson
Oct. 19, 1998

BLACK BLOC

LATE 1990s: SOME ACTIVISTS CONCLUDE THAT THERE'S NO ROOM IN THE DEMOCRATIC PARTY FOR THEM. THE ANTI-GLOBALIZATION MOVEMENT BECOMES MILITANT, PARTLY DUE TO THE INFLUENCE OF THE SO-CALLED BLACK BLOC ANARCHISTS. RADICAL ENVIRONMENTAL-ISTS BURN DOWN A SKI LODGE, A HOUSING DEVELOPMENT, AND PART OF AN AUTO DEALERSHIP.

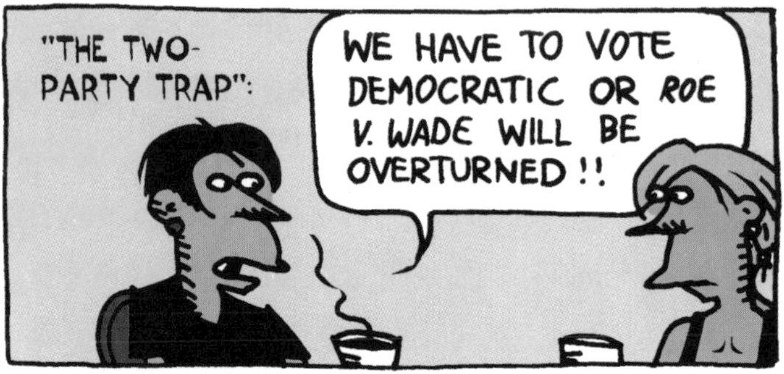
"THE TWO-PARTY TRAP":
WE HAVE TO VOTE DEMOCRATIC OR *ROE V. WADE* WILL BE OVERTURNED!!

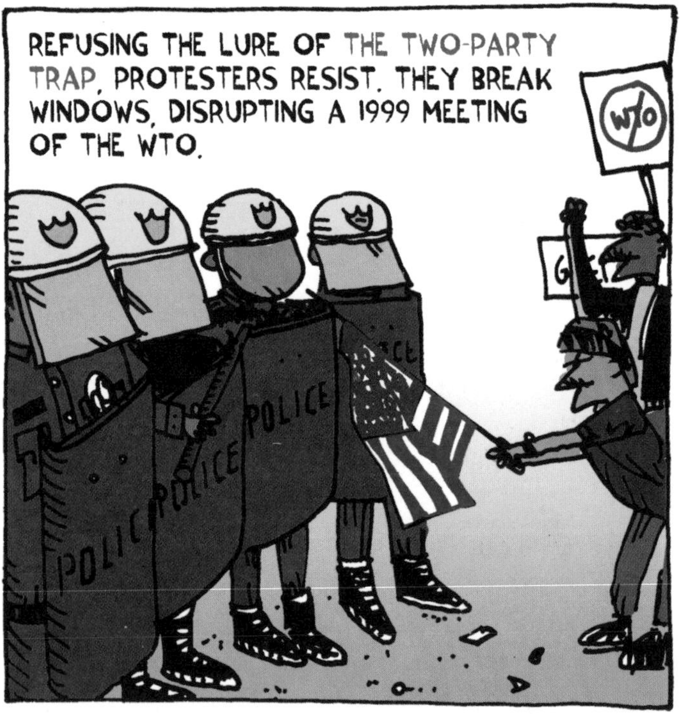
REFUSING THE LURE OF THE TWO-PARTY TRAP, PROTESTERS RESIST. THEY BREAK WINDOWS, DISRUPTING A 1999 MEETING OF THE WTO.
WTO
POLICE
POLICE
POLICE

[GORE AND BUSH ARE]

TWEEDLEDEE AND TWEEDLEDUM — THEY LOOK AND ACT THE SAME, SO IT DOESN'T MATTER WHICH YOU GET.

Ralph Nader

2000: CONSUMER ACTIVIST GADFLY RALPH NADER ATTACKS VICE PRESIDENT AL GORE FROM THE LEFT. GORE WINS THE POPULAR VOTE. BUT THE GOP-CONTROLLED U.S. SUPREME COURT SUSPENDS THE VOTE COUNT IN FLORIDA, WHERE THE TALLY IS TIGHT. GORE PASSIVELY ACCEPTS THE INSTALLATION OF USURPER GEORGE W. BUSH, THE MOST RADICAL RIGHT-WING REPUBLICAN OF THE MODERN POLITICAL ERA.

WE WILL STAND TOGETHER BEHIND OUR NEW PRESIDENT.

Al Gore

theguardian

JAN. 29, 2001

Florida 'recounts' make Gore winner

Al Gore, not George Bush, should be sitting in
...sident of the

"Nader's ego was so inflated... self-serving... his second futile go-around."
— ORLANDO SENTINEL FEB. 5, 2001

2001: MAINLINE DEMOCRATS BLAME NADER FOR GORE'S LOSS.

THEY CONVINCE THE MEDIA, AND MOST DEMOCRATS, THAT NADER SPLIT THE PROGRESSIVE VOTE.

2008: LONG YEARS OF BUSH, PERPETUAL WAR, AND LEGALIZED TORTURE ECLIPSE THE LEFT-CENTER DEBATE. THE LEFT IS GONE. THE CENTER-RIGHT DEMOCRATS ARE ALL THAT REMAIN.

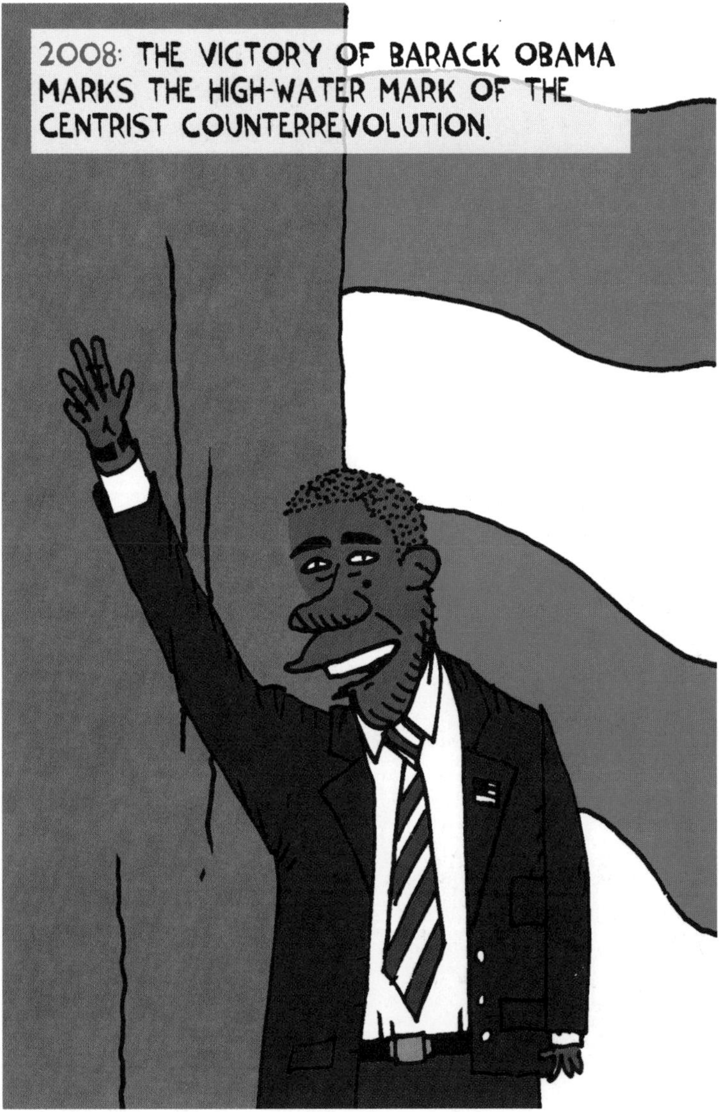
2008: THE VICTORY OF BARACK OBAMA MARKS THE HIGH-WATER MARK OF THE CENTRIST COUNTERREVOLUTION.

LIKE JIMMY CARTER, OBAMA GOVERNS TO THE RIGHT OF DEMOCRATIC PREDECESSORS LIKE TRUMAN AND LBJ -- SOME REPUBLICANS TOO. IT'S HARD TO IMAGINE EVEN RICHARD NIXON, ORIGINATOR OF THE DOCTRINE OF "EXECUTIVE PRIVILEGE," EMBRACING ASSASSINATION DRONES OR THE NSA'S MASS COLLECTION OF COMMUNICATIONS OF LAW-ABIDING CITIZENS.

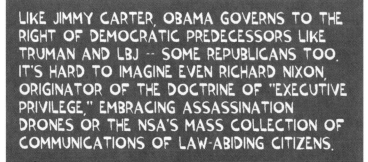

2009: THREE OF OBAMA'S EARLY MOVES ILLUSTRATE HOW FAR RIGHT THE DEMOCRATS, AND MAINSTREAM ELECTORAL POLITICS IN THE UNITED STATES, HAVE MOVED.

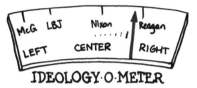

IDEOLOGY·O·METER

FIRST: OBAMA'S PERSONNEL PICKS. THE GLOBAL ECONOMIC MELTDOWN OF 2008-2009 CAUSED BANK FAILURES AND HOME FORECLOSURES AGAINST MILLIONS OF AMERICANS, MANY OF THEM ILLEGALLY.

OBAMA DIDN'T APPOINT A SINGLE TRADITIONAL LIBERAL TO HIS CABINET. EVEN CLINTON HAD PROGRESSIVE LABOR SECRETARY ROBERT REICH (WHOSE ADVICE HE MOSTLY IGNORED).

Paul Krugman
Nobel Prize - Winning
Economist who
predicted the 2008
Housing Crash
(No job offer from Obama)

SECOND: THE AFFORDABLE CARE ACT, ALSO KNOWN AS OBAMACARE. DURING THE CAMPAIGN, OBAMA HAD PROMISED A "SINGLE-PAYER" OPTION -- GOVERNMENT-RUN "SOCIALIZED MEDICINE," THE GLOBAL NORM.

ONCE IN OFFICE, HOWEVER, HE BREAKS THAT PROMISE. LIBERAL DEMOCRATIC LEGISLATORS DON'T COMPLAIN.

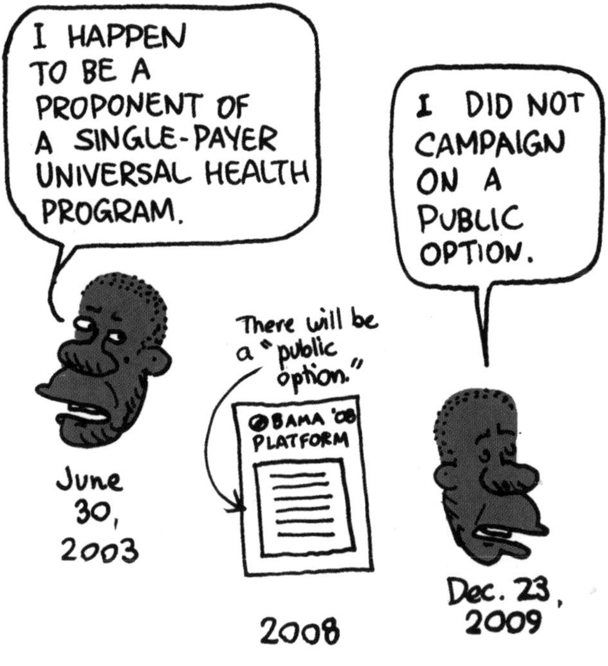
I HAPPEN TO BE A PROPONENT OF A SINGLE-PAYER UNIVERSAL HEALTH PROGRAM.
June 30, 2003
There will be a "public option."
OBAMA '08 PLATFORM
2008
I DID NOT CAMPAIGN ON A PUBLIC OPTION.
Dec. 23, 2009

THIRD: OBAMA USES FEDERAL MONEY TO BAIL OUT THE BANKS THAT CAUSED THE MELTDOWN WITH OUT-OF-CONTROL LENDING PRACTICES AND WIDESPREAD CORRUPTION. YET HE OFFERS LITTLE ASSISTANCE TO TENS OF MILLIONS OF INNOCENT VICTIMS OF THE CRISIS, WHO ARE LOSING THEIR JOBS AND THEIR HOMES.

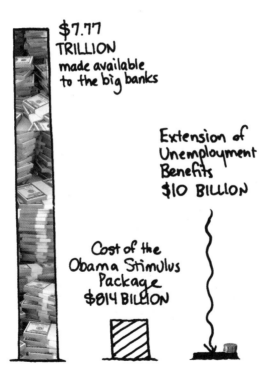

$7.77 TRILLION made available to the big banks

Extension of Unemployment Benefits $10 BILLION

Cost of the Obama Stimulus Package $814 BILLION

THE VOICES OF THE DISPOSSESSED ARE NOT HEARD IN OBAMA'S AMERICA. NEITHER MAJOR POLITICAL PARTY TALKS ABOUT INCOME INEQUALITY, WHICH HAS BEEN GROWING STEADILY SINCE THE 1970s.

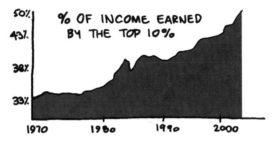

AVERAGE WAGES AND BENEFITS ARE STAGNANT OR SHRINKING. ALMOST ALL OF THE VAST WEALTH CREATED BY THE INTERNET BOOM IS GOING INTO THE POCKETS OF A TINY ELITE, THE SO-CALLED TOP 1%.

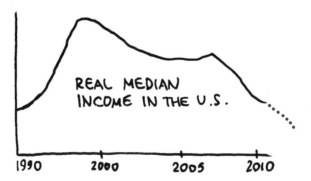

JOBS ARE SO HARD TO FIND THAT MILLIONS OF PEOPLE ARE GIVING UP LOOKING, DROPPING OUT OF THE WORKFORCE ENTIRELY. THEY'RE NO LONGER COUNTED AS OFFICIALLY UNEMPLOYED.

THEY'RE INVISIBLE.

RECENT COLLEGE GRADUATES EMERGE INTO A
BLEAK JOB MARKET, STAGGERING UNDER THE
BURDEN OF STUDENT LOANS THEY'LL NEVER BE
ABLE TO REPAY. BECAUSE CONGRESS HAS
REWRITTEN BANKRUPTCY LAWS IN FAVOR OF
THE BANKS, THOSE DEBTS ARE PERMANENT AND
CAN NEVER BE DISCHARGED.

Average
Student
Loan
Debt
$35,000
(Class
of
2015)

AMERICA ISN'T POOR. THERE'S ALWAYS
MONEY FOR WAR: TO INVADE AFGHANISTAN,
TO INVADE IRAQ, TO BUILD SO MANY NEW
MILITARY BASES THAT -- IT'S TRUE -- EVEN
THE PENTAGON MIGHT NOT KNOW HOW MANY
THERE ARE. WHAT THERE ISN'T IS MONEY FOR
AVERAGE PEOPLE. UNEMPLOYMENT BENEFITS
RUN OUT AFTER A FEW MONTHS. AFTER
THOSE PALTRY ASSISTANCE PAYMENTS END,
IT'S YOUR TOUGH LUCK, YOUR
PROBLEM, IF YOU'RE JOBLESS OR
POOR. YOU ARE ON YOUR OWN.

THERE'S NO MONEY TO FIX INFRASTRUCTURE,
EVEN THOUGH BRIDGES ARE COLLAPSING AND
THE NATION'S TRAIN SYSTEMS HAVE BEEN
ECLIPSED BY THOSE OF THIRD WORLD NATIONS.
NO MONEY FOR SCHOOLS, OR TEACHERS, OR
VETERANS, OR JOB TRAINING.

MILLIONS OF PEOPLE ARE ANGRY. AS HISTORY
SHOWS, OPPRESSED MASSES WON'T FOREVER
SUFFER IN SILENCE. IT'S ONLY A MATTER OF
TIME BEFORE THE DELUGE.

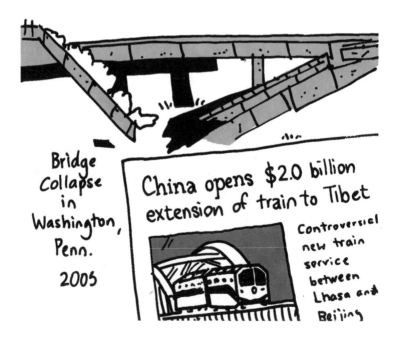

Bridge
Collapse
in
Washington,
Penn.
2005

China opens $2.0 billion
extension of train to Tibet

Controversial
new train
service
between
Lhasa and
Beijing

BERNIE'S MOMENT:
THE RISE AND
FALL OF OCCUPY

FALL 2011: CONJURED INTO EXISTENCE AT THE SUGGESTION OF A LOW-CIRCULATION CANADIAN MAGAZINE, THE BARELY-ORGANIZED "OCCUPY WALL STREET" MOVEMENT CAPTURED THE IMAGINATION OF THE WORLD. WITHIN WEEKS, THERE WERE HUNDREDS OF SPONTANEOUS, LOOSELY AFFILIATED "OCCUPATIONS" OF PUBLIC SPACES AROUND THE UNITED STATES.

IN THE HEYDAY OF THE DEMOCRATIC PARTY, IN THE 1960s OR 1970s, A DEMOCRATIC PRESIDENT MIGHT HAVE TRIED TO BRING OWS INTO HIS PARTY'S BIG TENT. HE COULD HAVE TOURED "OCCUPIED" CITIES, ATTENDED DISCUSSIONS, AND INVITED THE BRIGHTEST ACTIVISTS TO JOIN HIS TEAM AS POLITICAL ADVISORS.

BUT NOT IN 2011. LIBERALS WERE BARELY
TOLERATED WITHIN THE DEMOCRATIC PARTY.

WHEN PARTY BIGWIGS TALKED TO THEM AT
ALL, IT WAS TO TELL THEM TO SHUT UP,
VOTE FOR US, WRITE US CHECKS, AND GO
AWAY.

IT WAS TO BE A SHORT RESPITE FROM
CORPORATISM. AS THE WEATHER TURNED
COLD, OBAMA'S DEPARTMENT OF HOMELAND
SECURITY COORDINATED A SIMULTANEOUS
SERIES OF VIOLENT POLICE ATTACKS TO
ERADICATE THE OCCUPY MOVEMENT.

THE MOVEMENT HAD BEEN PEACEFUL.
NEVERTHELESS, ACROSS THE NATION, RIOT
POLICE STORMED INTO THE ENCAMPMENTS.
SWINGING THEIR BATONS AND SPEWING
    PEPPER SPRAY, OBAMA'S
      STORMTROOPERS DROVE THE YOUNG
      IDEALISTS INTO THE NIGHT.

THE PROGRESSIVE VALUES OF CIVIL RIGHTS, INCOME EQUALITY, AND SOCIAL JUSTICE NO LONGER HAD A HOME IN AMERICA, INSIDE THE DEMOCRATIC PARTY, OR OUTSIDE OF IT,

RIDICULED, REVILED, REVIVED: THE SOCIALIST SENATOR FROM VERMONT

LET'S GO BACK A LITTLE.

FALL 2011: OCCUPY WALL STREET IS IN FULL SWING. A COALITION OF ANARCHISTS, DISENFRANCHISED LEFTISTS, LIBERTARIANS, AND OTHER FACTIONS OUTSIDE THE DEMOCRATIC-REPUBLICAN DUOPOLY, OCCUPIERS BELIEVE THAT THE TWO-PARTY SYSTEM IS IRREDEEMABLE, BECAUSE BOTH PARTIES ARE IN THRALL TO BIG CORPORATE CONTRIBUTORS.

HOWEVER, ONE NAME FROM (SORT OF) WITHIN THE ESTABLISHMENT KEEPS POPPING UP:

A SELF-DESCRIBED "DEMOCRATIC SOCIALIST," SANDERS HAS LONG BEEN RIDICULED AND MARGINALIZED BY THE MAINSTREAM POLITICAL CLASS AND ITS ALLIES IN THE MEDIA.

IT'S... NICE TO KNOW THAT POSITIONS YOU HAVE BEEN ADVOCATING FOR YEARS ARE NOW GETTING OUT TO MAIN STREET,

AND THAT MILLIONS OF PEOPLE ARE BEGINNING TO SAY:

ENOUGH IS ENOUGH.

Oct. 21, 2011

NOW THAT THE OLD BOLDFACE NAMES HAVE BEEN DISCREDITED AND LEFT-WING POLITICS ARE RESURGENT, SANDERS'S OUTSIDER STATUS GIVES HIM CREDIBILITY.

IN THE HEADY SPIRIT OF THIS NEW ERA, IN
WHICH LEFTIST IDEAS HAVE BEEN VINDICATED
BY THIS CRASHING FAILURE OF CAPITALISM,
SANDERS'S BIGGEST WEAKNESS HAS BECOME
HIS GREATEST STRENGTH.

COULD SANDERS BE THE INSIDE-WASHINGTON
CHAMPION THE 99% HAVE BEEN WAITING FOR?

Sanders Files 'Saving American Democracy
Amendment'   DEC. 8, 2011

ECONOMY

Bernie Sanders Introduces Bill To
Lift the Payroll Tax Cap, Ensuring
Full Social Security Funding For
Nearly 75 Years
                            AUG. 25, 2011

SPECIAL TOPIC

Bernie Sanders Says It Would Be A
'Good Idea' To Primary President
Obama
                            JULY 22, 2011

SANDERS, AGE 70 IN 2011, IS A POLITICAL ODD-BALL: A FIRST-TERM SENATOR FROM THE TINY, QUIRKY STATE OF VERMONT, A REMOTE, SPARSELY POPULATED PLACE KNOWN FOR HIPPIES, BEAUTIFUL TREES, BEN AND JERRY'S ICE CREAM, AND SOCIALIZED HEALTH CARE.

SANDERS'S IDEAL AMERICA, HE TELLS
INTERVIEWERS, WOULD REORGANIZE ITS
ECONOMY AND GOVERNMENT TO LOOK MORE
LIKE THE DEMOCRATIC SOCIALIST NATIONS OF
DENMARK, NORWAY, AND SWEDEN.

PROGRESSIVE TAX CODES SKEWED IN FAVOR
OF THE WORKING CLASS AGAINST THE RICH
WOULD FUND A GENEROUS SOCIAL SAFETY
NET.

GOVERNMENT WOULD PLAY AN ACTIVE ROLE IN PEOPLE'S LIVES, ESPECIALLY WHEN THEY NEED HELP. PUBLIC POLICY WOULD MITIGATE THE WORST EFFECTS OF LAISSEZ-FAIRE CAPITALISM.

BUSINESS WOULD BE MORE REGULATED. INCOME WOULD BE DISTRIBUTED MORE EVENLY.

POLLS SHOW THAT VOTERS LIKE THESE IDEAS. BUT THEY ARE CENSORED OUT OF "MAINSTREAM" POLITICAL DISCUSSION, EVEN WITHIN THE DEMOCRATIC PARTY.

A TALL, GRUFF PRESENCE WHO SPEAKS WITH A HEAVY BROOKLYN ACCENT, BERNIE SANDERS (I-VT) HAS EARNED RESPECT ON CAPITOL HILL DESPITE HIS CRITICS' REPEATED COMPLAINTS ABOUT HIS "SOCIALISM."

IN A DEEPLY DIVIDED CONGRESS, EVEN REPUBLICANS LIKE HIM:

I THINK HE'S VERY OUTSPOKEN IN TERMS OF WHERE HE IS IDEOLOGICALLY.

BUT... I FIND HIM TO BE ONE WHO'S WILLING TO SIT DOWN AND COMPROMISE.

Sen. Richard Burr
R-NC

SANDERS IS AMIABLE. YET HE CAN'T BE FULLY ACCEPTED BY THE POLITICAL ESTABLISHMENT IN WASHINGTON.

[BERNIE'S VIEWS] ARE NOT WHERE THE MAJORITY OF THE AMERICAN PEOPLE ARE.

Rep. Jim Himes
D-CT

HE ALSO CATCHES FLAK FROM THE LEFT DUE TO HIS SUPPORT FOR ISRAEL. LIKE MANY LEFTIES, HE SUPPORTS A TWO-STATE SOLUTION. HOWEVER, HE IS CRITICIZED FOR DELIVERING HIS ANALYSES OF THE PALESTINIAN-ISRAELI CONFLICT WITH MORE NUANCE, AND LESS PASSION, THAN HE BRINGS TO OTHER ISSUES.

AFTER PRESIDENT OBAMA RENEGED ON HIS CAMPAIGN PROMISE FOR A "SINGLE PAYER" OPTION IN OBAMACARE, SANDERS RAISED A RARE VOICE OF OPPOSITION FROM THE LEFT.

IF WE ARE GOING TO PROVIDE COMPREHENSIVE QUALITY CARE TO ALL OF OUR PEOPLE, THE ONLY WAY WE WILL DO THAT IS THROUGH A MEDICARE-FOR-ALL, SINGLE-PAYER SYSTEM.

THE INFORMATION DISCLOSED BY EDWARD SNOWDEN HAS BEEN EXTREMELY IMPORTANT IN ALLOWING CONGRESS AND THE AMERICAN PEOPLE TO UNDERSTAND THE DEGREE TO WHICH THE NSA HAS ABUSED ITS AUTHORITY AND VIOLATED OUR CONSTITUTIONAL RIGHTS.

HE WAS ALSO ONE OF THE FEW SENATORS TO OPPOSE THE NSA SURVEILLANCE OF ORDINARY AMERICANS REVEALED BY EDWARD SNOWDEN.

SEN. BERNIE SANDERS

I - Vermont

BUT SANDERS'S SUPPORT MOSTLY DERIVED
FROM HIS OWS-ESQUE TAKE ON THE ECONOMY
AND INCOME DISTRIBUTION. WOULD HE EXPLOIT
THE YEARNING OF PROGRESSIVE DEMOCRATS
TO TAKE ON THE DLC FACTION LED BY
HILLARY CLINTON?

PEOPLE THOUGHT THAT ROLE WOULD FALL TO
ELIZABETH WARREN, ANOTHER POPULIST WHO'D
BEEN THE SUBJECT OF PRESIDENTIAL
SPECULATION.

THERE IS NOBODY IN THIS COUNTRY WHO GOT RICH ON HIS OWN.

NOBODY.

NOW LOOK, YOU BUILT A FACTORY AND IT TURNED INTO SOMETHING TERRIFIC, OR A GREAT IDEA? GOD BLESS. KEEP A BIG HUNK OF IT. BUT PART OF THE UNDERLYING SOCIAL CONTRACT IS...YOU... **PAY FORWARD.**

Eliz.
Warren
Aug.
2011

THEN WARREN SAID SHE WOULDN'T RUN.
LIBERALS TURNED TO BERNIE. COULD HE,
WOULD HE, PICK UP AND REIGNITE THE
EXTINGUISHED TORCH OF THE DEMOCRATIC
LEFT?

"If you were to speak to any audience
in America and you say: there's something
wrong with our system when the crooks
on Wall Street, through their recklessness
and criminal behavior, are able to cause a
recession, which has resulted in so much
suffering to people, and then they get bailed
out by the American people, and then three
years later end up making more money than
they ever have before: PEOPLE GO NUTS!"

NO ONE HAD MORE CREDIBILITY ON THE POTENT ISSUE OF INCOME INEQUALITY THAN BERNIE.

"CORPORATE TAX REVENUE IN 2010 WAS 27% LOWER THAN 2000, EVEN THOUGH CORPORATE PROFITS ARE UP 60%."

PROFITS 60%

TAXES PAID TO I.R.S. 60%

"SINCE 2000, NEARLY 12 MILLION AMERICANS HAVE SLIPPED OUT OF THE MIDDLE CLASS AND INTO POVERTY."

EUGENE V. DEBS
SOCIALIST PARTY LEADER
1896

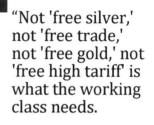

"Not 'free silver,' not 'free trade,' not 'free gold,' not 'free high tariff' is what the working class needs.

All of these 'free' things are like free coffins to be buried in.

Our slogan is 'Free the Tools of Production.'"

"When you make poor men -- when you permit the conditions to grow such that the poor man as such will be swayed by his sense of injury against the men who try to hold what they improperly have won, when that day comes, the most awful passions will be let loose and it will be an ill day for our country."

"The wealth in the United States was three times as much in 1910 as it was in 1890, and yet the masses of our people owned less in 1910 than they did in 1890. In the year 1916 the condition had become so bad that

...2% of the people in the United States owned 60% of the wealth in the country...

I propose that the surplus of all the big fortunes ...shall go into the United States' owner-ship."

90

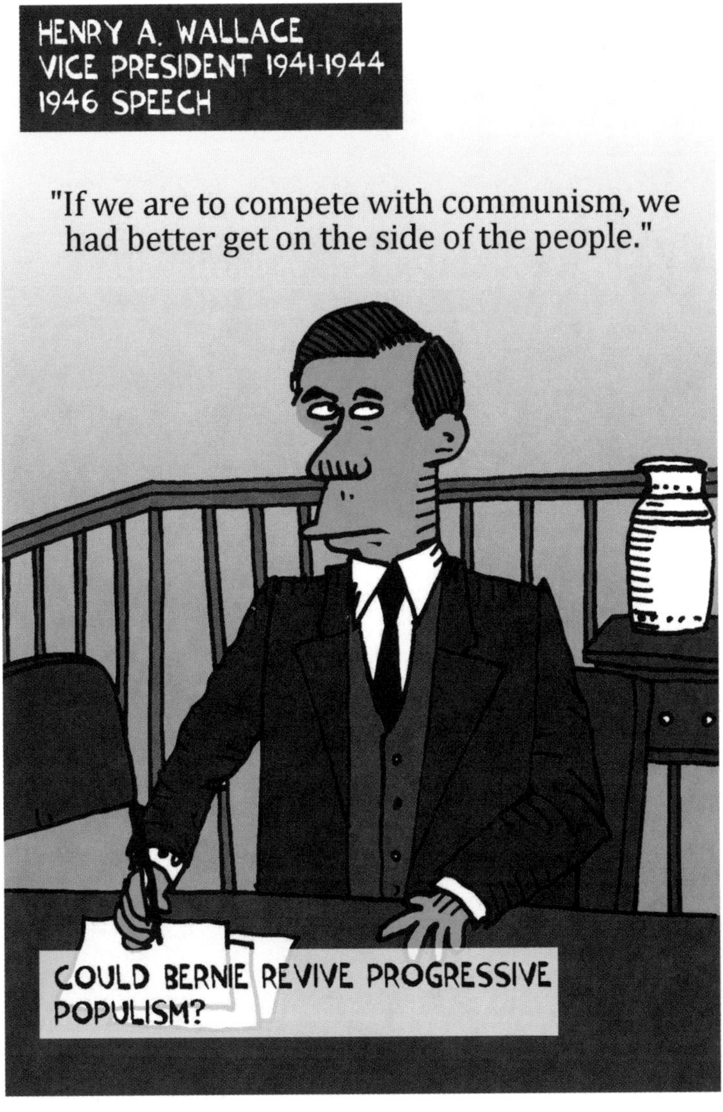
HENRY A. WALLACE
VICE PRESIDENT 1941-1944
1946 SPEECH
"If we are to compete with communism, we had better get on the side of the people."
COULD BERNIE REVIVE PROGRESSIVE POPULISM?

BERNIE ENJOYED THE UNIQUE CREDIBILITY THAT CAN COME TO THOSE WHO WANDER THE POLITICAL WILDERNESS FOR LONG ENOUGH TO COME TO BE SEEN AS A PROPHET.

"WASHINGTON IS DOMINATED BY BIG MONEY. SO YOU HAVE AN OVERWHELMING MAJORITY OF AMERICANS WHO BELIEVE THE WEALTHY SHOULD PAY THEIR FAIR SHARE. BUT YOU KNOW WHAT?"

"THE LOBBYISTS FROM WALL STREET AND CORPORATE AMERICA HAPPEN NOT TO AGREE WITH THAT, AND THEY'RE THE ONES THAT MAKE CAMPAIGN CONTRIBUTIONS."

"THEY ARE KNOCKING ON SENATORS' DOORS. THEY HAVE UNDUE INFLUENCE. THE VAST MAJORITY OF THE AMERICAN PEOPLE FEEL THAT WE SHOULD BE **TOUGH ON WALL STREET**.

UNFORTUNATELY, WALL STREET SPENDS HUNDREDS OF MILLIONS OF DOLLARS TO SUGGEST THAT WE LOOSEN UP."

MUSIC TO THE EARS OF THE MILLIONS OF AMERICANS WHO'D LOST THEIR JOBS AND HOMES, AND HADN'T RECEIVED ANY HELP FROM "THEIR" GOVERNMENT.

WHO WAS THIS MAN?

WHERE DID HE COME FROM?

WHY WAS HE UNIQUELY SITUATED TO ADDRESS PEOPLE'S ANGER OVER INCOME INEQUALITY, WHILE THE REST OF THE POLITICAL ESTABLISHMENT REMAINED CLUELESS?

BORN INTO A FAMILY THAT DIDN'T SO MUCH LEAN LEFT AS NOT LEAN RIGHT, BERNIE SANDERS'S SOCIALISM WAS REINFORCED BY PERSONAL EXPERIENCE AND HARDENED BY HIS WORK WITHIN LOCAL AND FEDERAL GOVERNMENT.

GROWING UP WITHOUT LOTS OF MONEY, I DIDN'T HAVE TO HAVE A BOOK TO TELL ME HOW A FAMILY GETS BY WHEN THERE IS NOT A LOT OF MONEY. I SAW UNFAIRNESS. THAT WAS THE MAJOR INSPIRATION IN MY POLITICS.

SANDERS'S POLITICS HAVE REMAINED REMARKABLY CONSTANT THROUGHOUT HIS LIFE, THOUGH HE DOESN'T ALWAYS SEEM AWARE OF IT.

DO I HAVE THE SAME VIEWS AS 50 YEARS AGO? PROBABLY NOT. IN ESSENCE, IN MY HEART OF HEARTS, WHO I AM AS A PERSON AND MY POLITICAL VIEWS HAVE REMAINED **CONSISTENT**.

THERE WAS NO POLITICAL JOURNEY. THERE WAS, INSTEAD, A STARTLING STEADINESS, IMPERVIOUS TO THE SHIFTING WINDS OF IDEOLOGICAL FASHION.

BERNIE SANDERS WAS WAITING.

WAITING FOR THE POLITICAL
WINDS TO SHIFT IN HIS
DIRECTION.

CHILD OF THE
REVOLUTION

THE FIRST THING YOU HAVE TO UNDERSTAND ABOUT BERNIE SANDERS IS THAT HE WAS A PRODUCT OF THE 1960s.

BUT HE WASN'T A HIPPIE.

HIS YOUNG ADULTHOOD UNFOLDED DURING THIS DEFINING PERIOD FOR BABY BOOMERS, THE UNCONVENTIONAL YET FAMILIAR GENERATION THAT HAS DOMINATED CULTURE AND POLITICS OVER THE PAST HALF-CENTURY.

HE WAS A MEMBER OF A FAMILIAR BOOMER SUBCULTURE, A YOUNG, CLEAN-CUT ACTIVIST-INTELLECTUAL. THE INFLUENCE OF THE "COUNTERCULTURE" WAS IMPOSSIBLE TO RESIST, ESPECIALLY IN HIS ROMANTIC RELATIONSHIPS -- BUT HE WAS OUT TO CHANGE THE WORLD, NOT DROP OUT.

BERNARD SANDERS WAS BORN ON SEPTEMBER 8, 1941, IN BROOKLYN, NEW YORK, THE SON OF ELI AND DOROTHY (GLASSBERG) SANDERS.

BOTH OF HIS PARENTS WERE JEWISH. THEY LEANED LEFT, BUT NOT BY MUCH.

MY PARENTS VOTED DEMOCRATIC, BUT THEY WERE NEVER REALLY INVOLVED IN POLITICS.

TODAY, BERNIE IDENTIFIES AS A "DEMOCRATIC SOCIALIST," IN THE VEIN OF THE SCANDINAVIAN DEMOCRACIES WHOSE SOCIAL POLICIES AND FLATTER INCOME DISTRIBUTION HE CITES APPROVINGLY AS AN EXAMPLE THE U.S. SHOULD EMULATE.

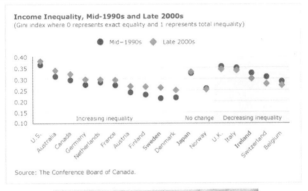

Income Inequality, Mid-1990s and Late 2000s
(Gini index where 0 represents exact equality and 1 represents total inequality)

● Mid−1990s ◆ Late 2000s

Increasing inequality · No change · Decreasing inequality

U.S., Australia, Canada, Germany, Netherlands, France, Austria, Finland, Sweden, Denmark, Japan, Norway, U.K., Italy, Ireland, Switzerland, Belgium

Source: The Conference Board of Canada.

WATCH THAT KICK: Bernie Sanders leads the field in the mile run as Lou Howort trails, a close second.

DESPITE HIS CONVENTIONALLY DEMOCRATIC PARENTS, BERNIE'S POLITICS WERE BAKED IN AT AN EARLY AGE.

ELI SANDERS EMIGRATED FROM POLAND IN 1917. TO BERNIE, HIS FATHER WAS A PERSONAL PARABLE ABOUT HOW WE'RE-ALL-ON-OUR-OWN CAPITALISM CAN BE UNFAIR AND CAPRICIOUS. ELI WAS THE ONLY MEMBER OF HIS FAMILY TO MAKE IT OUT OF EUROPE DURING THE EARLY 20th CENTURY. HIS OTHER RELATIVES DIED IN THE HOLOCAUST.

ELI WAS POOR. NO MATTER HOW HARD HE WORKED, HE COULDN'T ACHIEVE THE AMERICAN DREAM. UNLIKE OTHER RECENT IMMIGRANTS WHO COULD LEAN ON RELATIVES FOR HELP, ELI HAD NO ONE TO TURN TO FOR A LOAN OR A PLACE TO CRASH.

A PAINT SALESMAN WHO COMMUTED FROM BROOKLYN TO LONG ISLAND, ELI REMINDED BERNIE OF WILLY LOMAN, THE PATHETIC, DOOMED CHARACTER IN THE PLAY *DEATH OF A SALESMAN.*

LOMAN GETS FIRED AFTER PUTTING IN MORE THAN THREE DECADES WORKING FOR THE SAME COMPANY, NEVER HAVING EARNED ENOUGH TO SAVE.

DESPITE HIS FINANCIAL TROUBLES, ELI THOUGHT BERNIE'S GRANDFATHER, "A VERY STRONG SOCIALIST," WAS "ECCENTRIC."

DOROTHY SANDERS, NÉE GLASSBERG, WAS A BORN NEW YORKER. ONE OF SEVEN SISTERS, BERNIE'S MOTHER OFTEN GOT SICK, THE RESULT OF A CHILDHOOD BOUT OF RHEUMATIC FEVER THAT LEFT HER FRAIL. "MY MOTHER GREW UP IN THE BRONX. SHE WAS A VERY BEAUTIFUL WOMAN. SHE ALWAYS HAD A HEART PROBLEM," BERNIE REMEMBERS.

"SHE HAD A TEMPER. IT WAS NOT UNCOMMON FOR MY BROTHER AND I TO BE YELLED OUT, OR WORSE. THERE WAS A FAMOUS FAMILY STORY WHERE MY MOTHER MADE SOME EGGS FOR MY BROTHER LARRY FOR BREAKFAST. 'MOM, I DON'T WANT TO EAT THE EGGS.' WOMP! THE PILE OF EGGS WENT OVER HIS HEAD."

HE GOT ALONG WELL WITH HIS DAD.

"IT WAS A WARM RELATIONSHIP. HE WAS A VERY LOVING FATHER, VERY GREGARIOUS, MORE SO THAN MY MOTHER. HE LIKED PEOPLE, PROBABLY BECAUSE HE WAS A SALESMAN."

MONEY PROBLEMS STRESSED DOROTHY AND ELI'S MARRIAGE.

"THERE WERE TENSIONS ABOUT MONEY, WHICH I THINK IS IMPORTANT. THERE WAS NO SENSE OF LONG-TERM SECURITY. A SALESMAN, THINGS CAN GO UP AND THINGS CAN GO DOWN."

THE SANDERS' LIVED IN A ONE-BEDROOM APARTMENT AT 1525 EAST 26th STREET, AT THE CORNER OF KINGS HIGHWAY IN THE FLATBUSH SECTION OF BROOKLYN.

EVEN IN TODAY'S GENTRIFYING NEW YORK CITY, THE FRONT ENTRANCE IS SCARRED BY GRAFFITI. A JEWISH NEIGHBORHOOD AT THE TIME, FLATBUSH IS NOW MORE DIVERSE. IT'S STILL LESS THAN PROSPEROUS.

BEGINNING IN 1955, BERNIE ATTENDED P.S. 197 ELEMENTARY SCHOOL IN THE MIDWOOD SECTION OF BROOKLYN. HE WAS A STRIVER.

"I WAS A GOOD BASKETBALL PLAYER. MY ELEMENTARY SCHOOL WON THE BROOKLYN CHAMPIONSHIP IN A PRETTY COMPETITIVE ENVIRONMENT. I WAS THE STAR RUNNER."

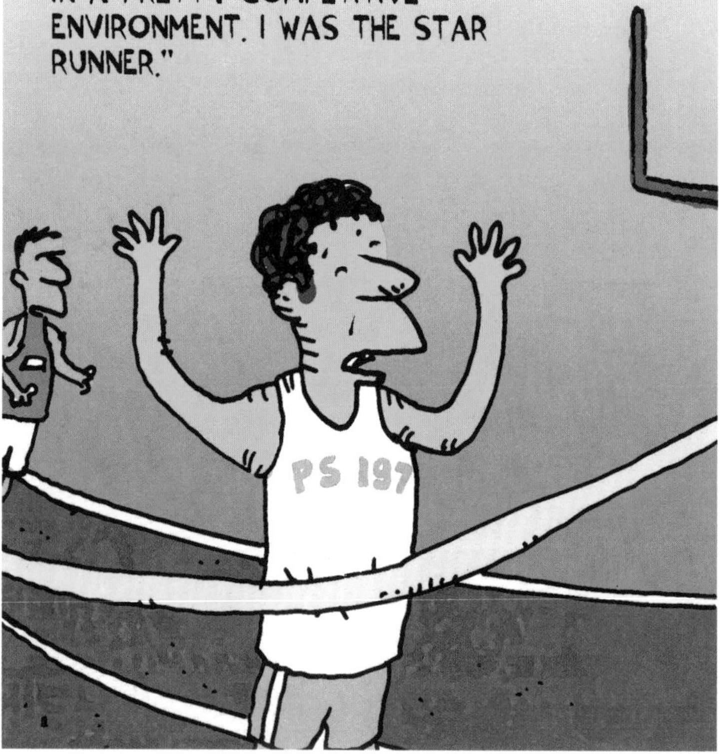
PS 197

BERNIE MADE HIS MARK IN SPORTS. EVEN SO, HE SUFFERED HIS SHARE OF SETBACKS.

I MADE THE JUNIOR VARSITY AND HALFWAY THROUGH I WAS CUT, WHICH WAS VERY TRAUMATIC FOR ME. THE UNIFORM, I WAS NUMBER 10. THAT WAS 60 YEARS AGO. THINK I'VE FORGOTTEN? DOESN'T MEAN A THING TO ME! THE SON OF A BITCH CUT ME!!

GO Knights!

MADISON 10

HE WAS ACTIVE IN BOY SCOUTS. HIS
MOTHER WAS A CUB SCOUT DEN MOTHER.
HIGHEST RANK: STAR.

"I WENT TO BOY SCOUT CAMP FOR A
NUMBER OF YEARS, AND IT WAS A REALLY
GOOD EXPERIENCE."

DETERMINED TO MAKE SOMETHING OF HIMSELF AND GET OUT OF FLATBUSH, HE WORKED HARD AT JAMES MADISON HIGH SCHOOL. WITH 5,000 STUDENTS, IT WAS EASY TO GET LOST IN THE SHUFFLE. FOR BERNIE AND OTHER HIGH ACHIEVERS, THE SCALE OF THE SCHOOL MOTIVATED THEM TO WORK HARDER.

113

THE NEIGHBORHOOD REINFORCED BERNIE'S POLITICS. HE WALKED TO SCHOOL WITH WALTER BLOCK, NOW AN ECONOMICS PROFESSOR AT LOYOLA. BLOCK REMEMBERS FLATBUSH AS "PRETTY PINKISH," I.E., POLITICALLY SYMPATHETIC TO SOCIALISM AND COMMUNISM, EVEN DURING THE MCCARTHY ERA.

DEFEND THE WORKING CLASS!

STR
BA CPUSA
Rally

SANDERS WAS OBSESSED WITH THE BROOKLYN DODGERS.

Brooklyn DODGERS

"WE LEARNED TO DO ARITHMETIC BY CALCULATING, IF GIL HODGES WAS BATTING .285 AND HE WENT ONE FOR THREE, WHAT WAS HIS NEW AVERAGE?"

BERNIE'S CHILDHOOD WAS ALL ABOUT SPORTS. HE WAS ON A TEAM THAT WON A STATE BASKETBALL CHAMPIONSHIP. ONE OF THE FASTEST LONG-DISTANCE RUNNERS IN THE BOROUGH OF BROOKLYN, HE ALSO BECAME CAPTAIN OF THE TRACK AND THE CROSS-COUNTRY TEAMS.

"I ALWAYS HAD GOOD ENDURANCE. ONE OF THE BETTER LONG-DISTANCE RUNNERS. NOT A SUPERSTAR, BUT I CAME IN THIRD PLACE IN THE MILE ONE YEAR, OFTEN WOULD WIN CROSS-COUNTRY MEETS."

"I SPENT ALL MY TIME PLAYING BALL. WE PLAYED BASEBALL AND BASKETBALL AND FOOTBALL AND PUNCHBALL AND STICKBALL. IT WAS ALL WE DID."

HIS PHYSICAL STRENGTH ALLOWED HIM
TO LIVE UP TO HIS IDEALS.

"WHEN I WAS A KID, FOR WHATEVER
REASON, INSTINCTIVELY, I ALWAYS
SIDED WITH THE UNDERDOG. WHEN
SOME OF THE BIG KIDS WOULD PICK
ON THE LITTLE KIDS, I WAS THERE WITH
THE LITTLE KIDS. I'VE NEVER LIKED
BULLYING, THE STRONGER AGAINST
THE WEAKER. WHERE THAT CAME FROM
I CANNOT TELL YOU."

HE WROTE FOR THE SCHOOL PAPER AND READ WORKS WITH A POLITICAL BENT: FREUD, PAINE, AND THE WORKS OF THE SEMINAL CONSERVATIVE EDMUND BURKE. BURKE, HE THOUGHT, WAS INTELLECTUALLY INFERIOR TO PAINE.

HE LOST HIS FIRST POLITICAL CAMPAIGN. WHEN BERNIE RAN FOR STUDENT BODY PRESIDENT, HE CAME IN LAST.

THIRD OUT OF THREE!

STILL, IT WASN'T A TOTAL LOSS. HE WOUND UP PRESIDENT OF HIS CLASS -- AND INFLUENCED THE WINNER. LARRY SANDERS: "THE STUDENT WHO WON ENDED UP ADOPTING BERNIE'S POLICY ABOUT RAISING MONEY FOR KOREAN ORPHANS."

SANDERS GRADUATED FROM HIGH SCHOOL DURING THE DOLDRUMS OF EISENHOWER'S SECOND TERM AS PRESIDENT. HE VISITED HARVARD AND BROWN. THEY TURNED HIM DOWN. IN ANY CASE, HIS MOTHER'S HEALTH WAS FAILING. HE STAYED CLOSE TO HOME TO CARE FOR HER AND FOLLOWED HIS BROTHER LARRY, WHO HAD GONE TO BROOKLYN COLLEGE.

MY BROTHER... INTRODUCED ME TO POLITICS.

THINGS WEREN'T GOOD AT HOME.

AS USUAL, THE PROBLEM WAS MONEY.

"THE CLASH IN MY FAMILY WAS THAT MY MOTHER WAS AN AMERICAN. SHE LOOKED AT THE WORLD DIFFERENTLY. SHE WAS OPTIMISTIC."

"MY FATHER CAME TO THIS COUNTRY WITH NOTHING. ECONOMICALLY, WHAT ALWAYS MOTIVATED HIM WAS SECURITY, THAT IS, NOT LOSING WHAT HE HAD. MY MOTHER WANTED MORE MONEY AND WANTED HIM TO GET A DIFFERENT JOB OR EXPAND WHAT HE WAS DOING. HE WAS VERY FRUGAL. BUT IF HE TRIED TO DO THAT, WE WOULD LOSE WHAT WE HAD."

"WE WERE LOWER-MIDDLE CLASS BUT THERE WAS NEVER A QUESTION OF WHETHER THERE WAS FOOD ON THE TABLE OR NOT. WE LIVED IN A RENT-CONTROLLED APARTMENT. THAT DIFFERENCE IN ATTITUDE CAUSED A LOT OF CONFLICTS."

EAGER TO ESCAPE THE FIGHTING, BERNIE MOVED OUT INTO THE CRAMPED THIRD-FLOOR ATTIC OF WHAT HAD ORIGINALLY BEEN DESIGNED AS A SINGLE-FAMILY HOME ON EAST 21st STREET, NEAR HIS PARENTS' PLACE. HE PAID $80 A MONTH.

"I HAD TO BE VERY CAREFUL NOT TO HIT MY HEAD ON THE CEILING."
--ROOMMATE STEVE SLAVIN

BERNIE AND HIS ROOMIE HUNG AROUND LISTENING TO RECORDS, EATING ICE CREAM, AND GEEKING OUT ON POLITICS. THEY DISCUSSED SUPREME COURT CASES, PARTICULARLY THE SEMINAL CASE OF *MARBURY V. MADISON*, WHICH ESTABLISHED THE JUDICIARY AS THE DISCRETE THIRD BRANCH OF AMERICAN GOVERNMENT.

A YEAR AFTER MOVING INTO HIS FIRST PLACE, BERNIE'S MOM UNDERWENT A SECOND OPERATION ON HER HEART, A PRECURSOR OF OPEN-HEART SURGERY.

THE PROCEDURE MADE THINGS WORSE, AND SHE DIED. DOROTHY WAS 46.

BERNIE WAS DEVASTATED.

AS IT HAD BEEN FOR HER HUSBAND, THE AMERICAN DREAM WAS A BITTER CHIMERA FOR DOROTHY.

"MY MOTHER WANTED TO OWN HER OWN HOME, WHICH SHE NEVER LIVED TO SEE. NEVER HAPPENED."

"SENSITIVITY TO CLASS WAS IMBEDDED IN ME THEN QUITE DEEPLY."

MOURNING HIS MOTHER, BERNIE WAS NOW FREE TO LEAVE BROOKLYN. IN 1961, HE APPLIED TO HARVARD BUT WAS AGAIN REJECTED. SO HE TRANSFERRED AS A SOPHOMORE TO THE UNIVERSITY OF CHICAGO, A MORE PRESTIGIOUS INSTITUTION THAN BROOKLYN COLLEGE. TO PAY THE HIGHER TUITION, HE WORKED IN THE SUMMERTIME, TOOK OUT A LOAN, AND PROBABLY RECEIVED A SCHOLARSHIP.

TUITION WAS A FRACTION OF WHAT IT IS TODAY. I WASN'T OVERWHELMED BY THE COST OF THE SCHOOL.

always with the political points!

125

DURING HIS COLLEGE YEARS THE POLITICS HE'D
ACQUIRED VIA EXPERIENCE IN BROOKLYN WERE
FLESHED OUT BY SOPHISTICATED THEORETICAL
CONSTRUCTS.

THE CITY, CAPITAL OF THE INDUSTRIAL MIDWEST AND
A CESSPOOL OF LOCAL POLITICAL CORRUPTION,
HONED BERNIE'S LEFT POLITICS. SO DID HIS
PROFESSORS. EVEN DURING THE ANTI-COMMUNIST
WITCH HUNTS OF THE '50s, "U OF C WAS KNOWN AS
A HOTBED OF RADICALISM," REMEMBERS SALLY COOK,
WHO GRADUATED IN 1965.

MARX EXPLAINS
THE TENDENCY
OF WEALTH AND
POWER TO
AGGREGATE INTO
MONOPOLISTIC
ENTITIES UNDER
CAPITALISM.

MUCH OF BERNIE'S EDUCATION TOOK PLACE OUT IN THE STREETS. "RADICALIZED BY THE GRINDING POVERTY HE SAW ... [ON] THE CITY'S SOUTH SIDE," HE JOINED THE CONGRESS OF RACIAL EQUALITY (CORE) AND THE STUDENT NONVIOLENT COORDINATING COMMITTEE (SNCC), ORGANIZATIONS AT THE FOREFRONT OF THE CIVIL RIGHTS MOVEMENT.

BERNIE DIDN'T SMOKE POT. HOWEVER, SOME OF HIS HIPPIE FRIENDS DID.

AN ENERGETIC, BRIGHT YOUNG MAN WITH A BIG SLOPPY SMILE, BERNIE ORGANIZED SIT-IN PROTESTS AGAINST SEGREGATION OF CAMPUS HOUSING. HE GOT ARRESTED.

HE TRAVELED TO THE 1963 MARCH ON WASHINGTON FOR JOBS AND FREEDOM. HE BECAME A MEMBER OF THE YOUNG PEOPLE'S SOCIALIST LEAGUE, THE YOUTH AFFILIATE OF THE SOCIALIST PARTY OF AMERICA.

BERNIE SPENT SEVERAL MONTHS IN 1964
WORKING ON AN ISRAELI KIBBUTZ, A ZIONIST
WORKING COMMUNITY ORGANIZED AROUND
SOCIALIST PRINCIPLES.

"BEING JEWISH HAD SOMETHING TO DO WITH
[MY POLITICS]. CERTAINLY THE HOLOCAUST
HAD A HUGE IMPACT UPON ME AND PEOPLE
MY AGE WHILE GROWING UP. WE WERE ALL
MINDFUL OF FAMILY MEMBERS WHO HAD BEEN
KILLED, AND UNDERSTANDING WHAT RACISM IS
ABOUT AND WHAT DEMAGOGUERY WAS
ABOUT."

THOUGH AMERICA'S INTERVENTION IN VIETNAM HAD BARELY BEGUN, THERE WAS A MILITARY DRAFT. BERNIE APPLIED FOR CONSCIENTIOUS OBJECTOR STATUS, ARGUING THAT AS A PACIFIST HE SHOULDN'T HAVE TO GO TO WAR. BY THE TIME HIS C.O. APPLICATION CAME UP, IT WAS 1967 AND THE WAR WAS ESCALATING -- BUT HE WAS 26, TOO OLD TO BE DRAFTED ANYWAY.

ON JUNE 13, 1964, SANDERS GRADUATED FROM THE UNIVERSITY OF CHICAGO WITH A B.A. IN POLITICAL SCIENCE. HE'D FALLEN IN LOVE WITH HIS COLLEGE GIRLFRIEND DEBORAH SHILING, THE DAUGHTER OF A SUCCESSFUL PULMONOLOGIST. ON SEPTEMBER 6, THEY GOT MARRIED IN THE GARDEN OF HER PARENTS' HOUSE IN BALTIMORE.

WHAT HAPPENED NEXT WOULDN'T SURPRISE
ANYONE WHO LIVED THROUGH THE 1960s, WHEN
TRADITIONAL SEXUAL MORES AND SOCIETAL
EXPECTATIONS WERE GIVING WAY TO GREATER
FREEDOM AND EXPERIMENTATION.

THE SANDERS' MOVED TO A CONVERTED SUGAR
SHACK IN MIDDLESEX, A VILLAGE NEAR THE
VERMONT CAPITAL OF MONTPELIER. IT WAS
RUSTIC, WITH RUNNING WATER BUT NO
ELECTRICITY. BUT IT WAS INCREDIBLY CHEAP:
$2,500 BOUGHT THEM 85 ACRES OF LAND IN ONE
OF THE MOST PICTURESQUE REGIONS OF THE
COUNTRY.

THEIR MARRIAGE QUICKLY COLLAPSED. AFTER A
TRIP TO EUROPE, THE COUPLE RETURNED TO
VERMONT IN 1966 AND DIVORCED. BERNIE WAS
25. WHAT WENT WRONG? NO ONE, INCLUDING
FRIENDS, WILL TALK ABOUT IT.

DEBORAH WON'T COMMENT ABOUT HER
MARRIAGE TO BERNIE, BUT WHATEVER LED TO
THE BREAKUP, ANY RANCOR HAS FADED. SHE
SAYS THAT SHE AND HER SECOND HUSBAND
BOUGHT OUT BERNIE'S SHARE OF THE
MIDDLESEX PROPERTY AND THAT SHE'LL VOTE
FOR HER EX.

BERNIE MOVED IN WITH A GIRLFRIEND, SUSAN MOTT. MOTT BECAME PREGNANT AND, ON MARCH 21, 1969, BERNIE'S FIRST SON, LEVI, WAS BORN. (HE'S NOW 46.)

MARTHA ABBOTT, A LONG-TIME SANDERS ALLY, REMEMBERS THAT BERNIE ADORED LEVI. AS A FREELANCE WRITER SHORT OF CASH, POVERTY MADE LIFE DIFFICULT...AGAIN.

HE WAS VERY COMMITTED TO BEING A PARENT. AND HE SCRAPED THE MONEY TOGETHER TO TAKE CARE OF HIM.

Martha Abbott, Sanders ally

A POLITICAL OUTSIDER GOES INSIDE

STREET PROTEST FADED AWAY DURING THE 1970s. THE LEFT EXPERIMENTED WITH NEW TACTICS TO TRY TO EFFECT SOCIAL AND POLITICAL CHANGE.

ON THE RADICAL FRINGE, MILITANT GROUPS LIKE THE BLACK PANTHERS, THE WEATHERMEN, AND THE RED ARMY FACTION EMBRACED VIOLENT IMAGERY AND ATTACKS.

BEGINNING WITH THE FEMINIST AND GAY LIBERATION MOVEMENTS, LIBERALS MIGRATED INTO "IDENTITY POLITICS."

PROGRESSIVES LIKE BERNIE TURNED THEIR ATTENTION TO THIRD PARTIES WORKING WITHIN THE ELECTORAL SYSTEM.

1971: SANDERS JOINED VERMONT'S LIBERTY UNION PARTY. THE LUP, WHICH STILL EXISTS, DEFINES ITSELF AS "NONVIOLENT SOCIALIST" AND FORMED AS A RESPONSE TO THE ANTI-VIETNAM WAR AND "PEOPLE'S PARTY" MOVEMENTS.

SANDERS RAN AS THE LIBERTY UNION CANDIDATE FOR GOVERNOR OF VERMONT IN 1972. AS YOU'D EXPECT, THE UNKNOWN 30-YEAR-OLD ON THE PLATFORM OF A TINY THIRD PARTY GOT TROUNCED.

TWO YEARS LATER, HOWEVER, WITH CONSERVATIVES DISCREDITED BY THE WATERGATE SCANDAL AND THE RESIGNATION OF PRESIDENT NIXON, HE DID BETTER. IN HIS 1974 SENATE RACE, HE FINISHED THIRD, WITH 4.1% OF THE VOTE.

BY 1979, LIBERTY UNION SEEMED TO BE LOSING STEAM, SO BERNIE LEFT TO GO BACK TO WORK AS A WRITER.

HE ALSO TOOK A JOB AS DIRECTOR OF THE NONPROFIT AMERICAN PEOPLE'S HISTORICAL SOCIETY, WHERE HE PRODUCED A DOCUMENTARY FILM ABOUT THE EARLY 20th-CENTURY SOCIALIST LEADER AND PRESIDENTIAL CANDIDATE EUGENE V. DEBS.

ONE OF MANY NOW-FORGOTTEN ICONS OF AMERICAN SOCIALISM, SANDERS'S IDOL DEBS WAS JAILED FOR HANDING OUT PACIFIST LEAFLETS DURING WORLD WAR I.

IN AN OFT-CITED DECISION ON FREE SPEECH, SUPREME COURT JUSTICE OLIVER WENDELL HOLMES RULED AGAINST DEBS'S RIGHT TO OPPOSE WAR, WRITING: "THE MOST STRINGENT PROTECTION OF FREE SPEECH WOULD NOT PROTECT A MAN FALSELY SHOUTING FIRE IN A THEATER AND CAUSING A PANIC."

IN 1969, HOWEVER, THAT DECISION WAS REVERSED. SO, ACTUALLY, YOU DO HAVE THE RIGHT TO SHOUT FIRE IN A CROWDED THEATER.

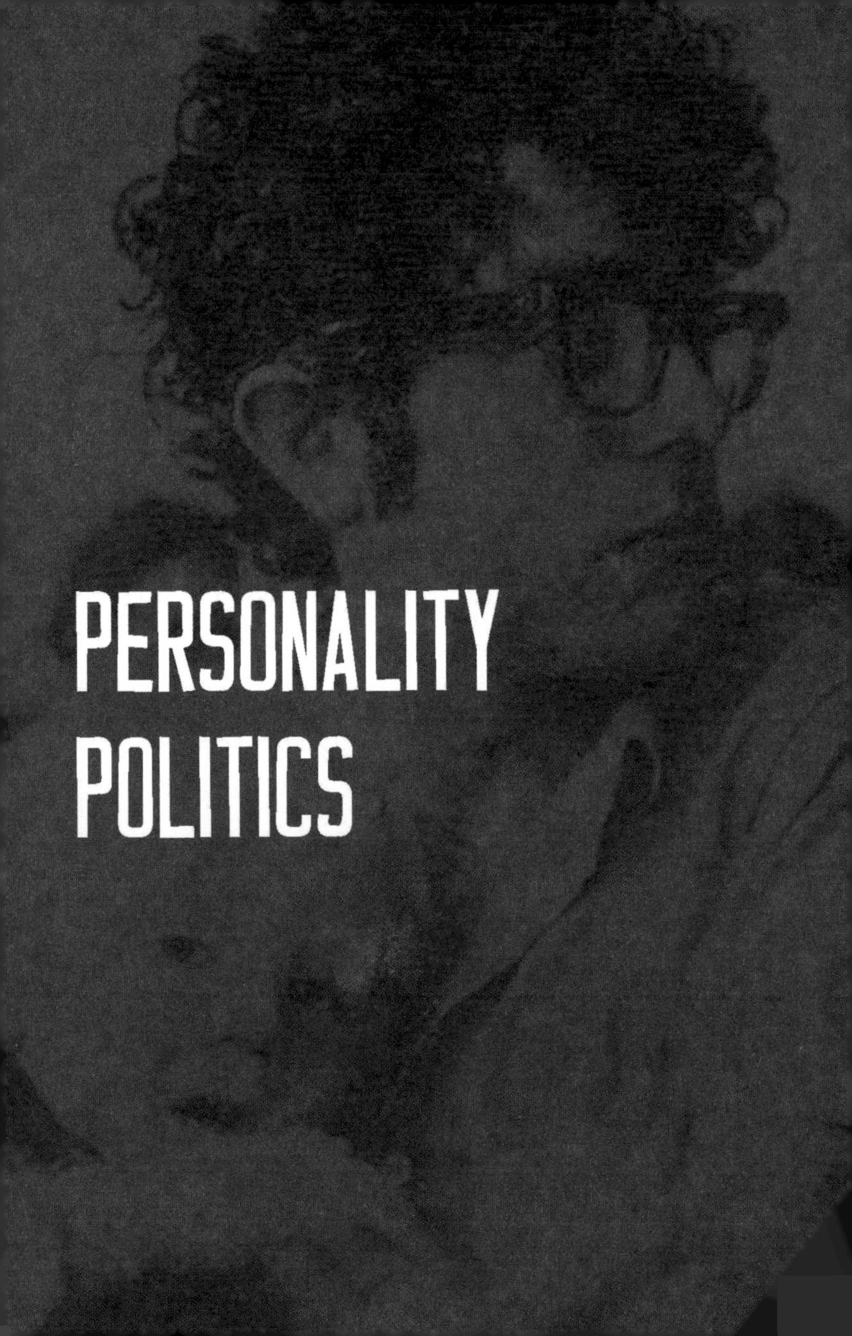
PERSONALITY
POLITICS

IN 1981 BERNIE'S FRIEND AND THEN-ROOMMATE, THE RELIGION AND PHILOSOPHY PROFESSOR RICHARD SUGARMAN OF THE UNIVERSITY OF VERMONT, TOLD BERNIE HE SHOULD RUN FOR MAYOR OF BURLINGTON, VERMONT.

BERNIE SANDERS CAME FROM LEFT-OF-CENTER JUDAISM, WHICH LEANS TOWARD THE SECULAR/REFORM SIDE.

FOR REFORM JEWS IN GENERAL, SOCIAL CONSCIOUSNESS AND CONCERN FOR THE PLIGHT OF THE POOR AND OPPRESSED IS A PRIORITY AND A RELIGIOUS OBLIGATION.

BERNIE DOESN'T LIKE TO TALK ABOUT HIS PERSONAL HISTORY. IT'S NOT THAT HE HAS SOMETHING TO HIDE -- IF THERE WAS A SKELETON IN HIS CLOSET, FOUR DECADES IN POLITICS WOULD HAVE ROOTED IT OUT.

HE THINKS IT'S A DISTRACTION FROM WHAT MATTERS AND WHAT HE CARES ABOUT: IDEAS. PROBLEMS AND HOW TO SOLVE THEM ARE HIS OBSESSIONS.

I'LL TELL YOU WHY [I'M TIGHT-LIPPED ABOUT MY PERSONAL LIFE].

WHAT WE HAVE IN THIS COUNTRY IS LOOKING AT POLITICS AS IF IT WERE A SOAP OPERA OR A BASEBALL GAME.

PERSONALITY POLITICS ANNOY HIM.

"DONALD TRUMP CALLED YOU THE FOLLOWING THING. HOW DO YOU RESPOND TO DONALD TRUMP?"

WHO GIVES A SHIT? THAT'S PERSONALITY. WHO CARES?

"GEORGE W. BUSH IS A DECENT GUY. GOOD SENSE OF HUMOR. HE IS A GOOD FAMILY GUY. HE IS A FUN GUY. HIS WIFE IS A VERY NICE PERSON. HE WAS THE **WORST PRESIDENT** IN THE MODERN HISTORY OF AMERICA! TO THE DEGREE THAT YOU FOCUS ON HIS PERSONALITY, THEN YOU ARE MINIMIZING DEMOCRACY WHAT IS SUPPOSED TO BE ABOUT."

ONE ASPECT OF HIS YOUTH BERNIE IS HAPPY TO DISCUSS IS THE TRAUMA OF GROWING UP POOR. HE HAS NEVER FORGOTTEN WHAT IT FELT LIKE TO HAVE TO WORRY ABOUT MAKING THE RENT, TO LIVE IN FEAR OF THE BILLS, TO PAY TO KEEP THE LIGHTS ON EVERY MONTH.

THERE HAD TO BE A BETTER WAY TO LIVE, HE THOUGHT AS A KID -- A MORE COMPASSIONATE ECONOMIC SYSTEM, A MORE RESPONSIVE POLITICAL CLASS.

BERNIE TOOK ON THE CAMPAIGN WITH HIS
USUAL DETERMINATION AND EARNESTNESS.
RUNNING AS AN INDEPENDENT, HE DEPLOYED
FIERY POPULISM WHILE DECRYING A
PROPOSAL TO TURN THE OLD INDUSTRIAL
WATERFRONT INTO A RITZY CONDO AND
OFFICE TOWER DEVELOPMENT.

SANDERS'S SLOGAN, "BURLINGTON IS NOT
FOR SALE," TOOK OFF.

SANDERS WON AN INCREDIBLY NARROW TEN-VOTE VICTORY OVER THE SIX-TERM DEMOCRATIC INCUMBENT, GORDON PAQUETTE.

THE RESULTS STUNNED THE LOCAL POLITICAL ESTABLISHMENT.

IT WAS ONE OF THE GREAT UPSETS IN VERMONT POLITICAL HISTORY, AND OUR STATE IS OVER 200 YEARS OLD.

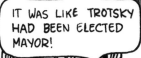

IT WAS LIKE TROTSKY HAD BEEN ELECTED MAYOR!

AT THE HEIGHT OF THE REAGAN REVOLUTION, ONE OF THE FEW SOCIALISTS TO EVER WIN ELECTED OFFICE IN U.S. HISTORY HAD BECOME THE ONLY INDEPENDENT MAYOR IN THE COUNTRY.

SANDERS WAS A POPULAR MAYOR, SERVING
FOUR TERMS. HE WAS ABLE TO GOVERN
WITHOUT DEMOCRATIC OR REPUBLICAN
PARTY ALLIANCES BECAUSE HIS SUPPORTERS
ON THE CITY COUNCIL FORMED A
"PROGRESSIVE COALITION,"

LATER FORMALIZED AS THE VERMONT
PROGRESSIVE PARTY. THE COALITION NEVER
ENJOYED MAJORITY CONTROL BUT HAD
ENOUGH VOTES TO PREVENT OVERRIDES OF
SANDERS'S VETOES.

SANDERS PRACTICED RETAIL POLITICS. HE
OVERSAW THE FIRST ATTEMPT BY A CITY
TO BUILD COMMUNITY-TRUST HOUSING.

Become a Homeowner!

The Burlington Community
Land Trust's **Old North End
Homeownership Program**
may help you become a
HOMEOWNER!

🏠 $12,500 off a home of your choice
in Burlington's Old North End

🏠 Downpayment assistance

🏠 Low mortgage rate starting at 6.05%
and 7.55% APR*

* 7.55% APR assumes 6.05% year 1; 6.55% year 2;
7.05% year 3 and 7.55% year 4-30

Qualified buyers must meet income guidelines and
share their appreciation with future homebuyers.

(TDD) for more

**HOMEOWNERSHIP
PROGRAM**

Old North End

VERMONTERS HATED THEIR LOCAL CABLE
COMPANY BECAUSE IT KEPT RAISING RATES,
SO HE SUED THEM AND WON A RATE CUT.

LEFTIES ARE OFTEN
ACCUSED OF FISCAL
PROFLIGACY, BUT
BERNIE BALANCED THE
CITY BUDGET.

THE SOCIALIST MAYOR
USED CAPITALIST
MEANS TO STIMULATE
BURLINGTON'S SLEEPY
ECONOMY,
HISTORICALLY BASED
ON LUMBER AND MILLS.

HE LURED A MINOR
LEAGUE BASEBALL
TEAM, THE VERMONT
REDS, TO BURLINGTON.

HE REPLACED THE LAKE
CHAMPLAIN WATER-
FRONT SCHEME HE'D
RUN AGAINST WITH A
DISTRICT INCLUDING
LONG PUBLIC BEACHES
AND BIKE PATHS, A
BOATHOUSE, PARKS,
AND A SCIENCE
CENTER.

1988: SANDERS DECIDED TO LEAVE THE MAYORALTY TO RUN FOR VERMONT'S SINGLE "AT LARGE" SEAT IN THE U.S. HOUSE OF REPRESENTATIVES. HE LOST TO THE REPUBLICAN LIEUTENANT GOVERNOR OF VERMONT 41% TO 38%, WITH THE DEMOCRAT TRAILING A DISTANT THIRD AT 19%.

DURING HIS LAST YEAR AS MAYOR, HE MARRIED HIS SECOND AND CURRENT WIFE, JANE O'MEARA. SHE HAD THREE CHILDREN FROM A PREVIOUS MARRIAGE. SANDERS'S CAMPAIGN LITERATURE EXPLAINS THAT HE DOESN'T DISTINGUISH BETWEEN LEVI AND HIS STEPCHILDREN, HEATHER, CARINA, AND DAVID.

AS THE 1980s "ME DECADE" GAVE WAY TO
THE 1990s, BERNIE FLIRTED WITH THE
POSSIBILITY OF BECOMING AN ACADEMIC,
LECTURING AT HARVARD AND HAMILTON
COLLEGE. BUT POLITICS CALLED AGAIN.

HE RAN FOR THE HOUSE AGAIN IN 1990. IN THIS
REMATCH, HE HANDILY DEFEATED HIS
OPPONENT 56% TO 40%, BECOMING THE FIRST
INDEPENDENT ELECTED TO THE HOUSE IN 40
YEARS.

BERNIE SPENT 16 YEARS IN THE HOUSE.
THERE, HIS VOTING RECORD WAS
IDEOLOGICALLY MIXED.

WHILE CRITICIZING REPUBLICANS FOR
GUTTING SOCIAL PROGRAMS, HE
SUPPORTED NRA-SPONSORED
LEGISLATION ON GUN RIGHTS -- NOT A
TYPICAL LIBERAL POSITION, BUT
REFLECTIVE OF HIS RURAL STATE, WHICH
IS HOME TO MANY HUNTERS.

BERNIE PROMOTED MAIN STREET OVER
WALL STREET, ACCUSING FEDERAL
RESERVE CHAIRMAN ALAN GREENSPAN OF
BEING OUT OF TOUCH AND IN THE
POCKET OF BIG BUSINESS. ON ISSUES OF
WAR AND MILITARISM, HOWEVER, REP.
SANDERS WAS LESS RELIABLY LEFT.

HE VOTED FOR INVADING AFGHANISTAN BUT AGAINST ATTACKING IRAQ. HE VOTED AGAINST THE USA PATRIOT ACT, WHICH AUTHORIZES MASS SURVEILLANCE OF ALL AMERICANS.

BUT HE REFUSED TO ENTERTAIN THE POSSIBILITY OF IMPEACHING PRESIDENT GEORGE W. BUSH.

"Before we talk about impeachment, it is imperative that [the] investigations be allowed to run their course."

STATEMENT ON IMPEACHMENT, 2007

IN 2006, SANDERS RAN FOR THE U.S. SENATE SEAT VACATED BY A RETIREMENT. WITH THE SUPPORT OF DEMOCRATIC PARTY OFFICIALS WHO SAID HE VOTED WITH THEIR PARTY "98% OF THE TIME," HE DEFEATED HIS REPUBLICAN RIVAL 2-1.

IF BERNIE WAS A FRINGE KOOK, HE WAS A POPULAR ONE. AT A TIME WHEN THE APPROVAL RATING FOR CONGRESS OVERALL FELL TO SINGLE DIGITS, IN 2011 HE WAS THE THIRD-MOST POPULAR SENATOR.

AS BERNIE JOINED THE SENATE IN 2007, THE BUSH YEARS WERE DRAWING TO A CLOSE. AMERICANS HAD TURNED AGAINST THE PERPETUAL WAR ON TERROR. THREATS FROM ABROAD WERE BEING SUPPLANTED BY DOMESTIC CONCERNS. THE HOUSING BUBBLE OF THE 2000s HAD BURST: BANKS WERE FAILING, FORECLOSURES WERE SKYROCKETING, AND MILLIONS OF AMERICANS WERE LOSING THEIR JOBS.

BUSH AND OBAMA RESCUED HUGE BANKS LIKE CHASE, BANK OF AMERICA, AND CITIBANK, THOSE ONCE DEEMED "TOO BIG TO FAIL," TO RESTORE LIQUIDITY TO CREDIT MARKETS.

BERNIE SANDERS RAILED AGAINST THE IDEA OF TRANSFERRING HUNDREDS OF BILLIONS OF TAX DOLLARS TO THE SAME CORPORATIONS THAT HAD CAUSED THE CRASH, WHILE LEAVING THE UNEMPLOYED ON THEIR OWN, WITH LITTLE TO NO HELP.

THERE IS A WHOLE LOT OF **ANGER** AND MISTRUST OF LARGE FINANCIAL INSTITUTIONS AND WALL STREET THAT CAUSED THE TERRIBLE, TERRIBLE RECESSION.

AND AT THE END OF THE DAY... CEOS ARE MAKING MORE THAN THEY EVER DID AND... BANKS ARE NOW CHARGING $5 ON DEBIT CARDS.

"THE COUNTRY'S SIX LARGEST FINANCIAL INSTITUTIONS [BANK OF AMERICA, CITIGROUP, JP MORGAN CHASE, WELLS FARGO, MORGAN STANLEY, AND GOLDMAN SACHS] HAVE NOW AMASSED ASSETS EQUAL TO MORE THAN 60% OF OUR GDP. THAT IS $9 TRILLION."

"THE FED, WITH **NO TRANS- PARENCY** AT ALL, IS LENDING OUT **TRILLIONS** OF DOLLARS. TO WHOM, WE DON'T KNOW; UNDER WHAT TERMS, WE DON'T KNOW, AS WELL."

BERNIE WAS ONE OF THE FEW MEMBERS OF
CONGRESS TO VOTE AGAINST THE BANK
BAILOUT. HE VOTED AGAINST OBAMA'S
NOMINATION OF TIM GEITHNER AS
TREASURY SECRETARY BECAUSE HE WAS
COZY WITH BANKERS.

AND HE VOTED AGAINST OBAMA'S
EXTENSION OF BUSH'S TAX CUTS FOR THE
WEALTHY, WHICH OTHERWISE WOULD HAVE
EXPIRED IN 2011.

THE RETURN OF
THE DEMOCRATIC
LEFT

AT THE HEIGHT OF THE OCCUPY WALL STREET MOVEMENT, BERNIE WAS RIDING HIGH IN THE POLLS. BUT HE DIDN'T WANT TO RUN FOR PRESIDENT.

I WOULD LIKELY END UP CAUSING A RIGHT-WING EXTREMIST TO BE PRESIDENT OF THE U.S.... IT WOULD LIKELY BE A FUTILE AND LOSING CAMPAIGN.

THERE WAS ANOTHER FACTOR: THE "INEVITABLE" HILLARY CLINTON. THE FORMER FIRST LADY, U.S. SENATOR, AND SECRETARY OF STATE HAD ALREADY ASSEMBLED A DAUNTING 2016 CAMPAIGN JUGGERNAUT THAT CAME AS CLOSE

TO UNBEATABLE AS ANY ATTEMPT TO CAPTURE THE DEMOCRATIC NOMINATION IN THE MEMORY OF PROFESSIONAL POLITICOS.

HILLARY HAD A VAST RESERVE OF CASH, SEASONED ADVISORS AND STAFFERS, AND THE SUPPORT OF THE DEMOCRATIC PARTY ESTABLISHMENT, INCLUDING THE SITTING PRESIDENT, WHOM SHE'D SERVED.

WOMEN VOTERS WERE EXCITED AT THE TANTALIZING
POSSIBILITY THAT THEY'D FINALLY SEE ONE OF
THEIR OWN ELECTED PRESIDENT.

EVEN WOMEN WHO THOUGHT HER TOO
CONSERVATIVE WERE WILLING TO OVERLOOK HER
POLITICS. SIMILAR EXCITEMENT AMONG AFRICAN
AMERICANS ("YES WE CAN") HAD PROPELLED
OBAMA TO TWO BIG WINS.

OLD, WHITE, AND MALE, SANDERS DIDN'T PLAY INTO
THIS IDENTITY POLITICS NARRATIVE.

WARMONGER,
WALL STREETER,
FREE TRADER.
I HATE EVERY-
THING HILLARY
STANDS FOR.

BUT: "FIRST
WOMAN
PRESIDENT
ELECTED."

THERE
IS
THAT...

SANDERS HAD OPENED HIS MIND TO RUNNING.

HE'D BEEN WATCHING HILLARY CAREFULLY. THE COUNTRY HAD SHIFTED LEFT, ESPECIALLY ON ISSUES RELATED TO ECONOMIC FAIRNESS AND JUSTICE. BUT HILLARY CLINTON WASN'T OFFERING ANYTHING NEW BEYOND THE SYMBOLISM OF A FIRST WOMAN PRESIDENT.

I DON'T WAKE UP EVERY MORNING THINKING ABOUT WHETHER I SHOULD BE PRESIDENT OF THE U.S.

CLINTON vs BUSH RE
POLITICAL DYNASTIES

BERNIE THOUGHT HILLARY NEEDED A PRIMARY CHALLENGER FROM THE LEFT TO ENGAGE HER -- SOMEONE WITH HIS PASSION FOR THE PROBLEMS OF THE POOR AND WORKING CLASS.

IDEALLY, SOMEONE ELSE WOULD STEP UP.

FORECLOSED

THOSE ISSUES HAVE TO BE DISCUSSED. AND IF NO ONE ELSE IS, I WILL DISCUSS THEM.

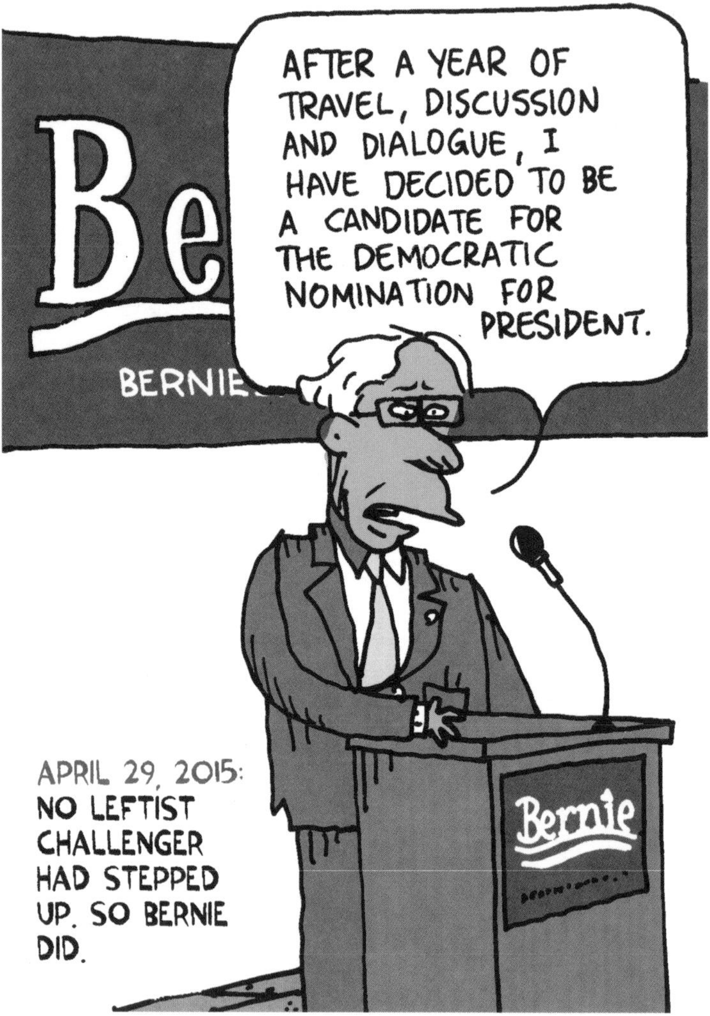
AFTER A YEAR OF TRAVEL, DISCUSSION AND DIALOGUE, I HAVE DECIDED TO BE A CANDIDATE FOR THE DEMOCRATIC NOMINATION FOR PRESIDENT.
Bernie
APRIL 29, 2015:
NO LEFTIST CHALLENGER HAD STEPPED UP. SO BERNIE DID.

RUNNING AS A DEMOCRAT
WAS A CONCESSION
TO FINANCIAL AND
POLITICAL REALITY.

IN THE YEAR
2015 AND 2016
THERE IS NOT
THE CAPABILITY
BY ANY STRETCH
OF THE
IMAGINATION TO
PUT TOGETHER
A SUCCESSFUL
THIRD-PARTY
EFFORT. I'M NOT
A BILLIONAIRE.

Net Worth: $700,000

AFTER A TENTATIVE LAUNCH, BIG
CROWDS TURNED UP AT BERNIE'S
RALLIES -- BIGGER THAN AT HILLARY'S.

THAT INCREASED HIS CONFIDENCE.

HERE, FOR THE FIRST TIME IN 40 YEARS, WAS A CANDIDATE RUNNING FOR THE DEMOCRATIC NOMINATION WHO WAS TALKING ABOUT BREAD-AND-BUTTER ISSUES, ABOUT FIGHTING FOR THE POOR AS WELL AS THE USUAL MYTHICAL "MIDDLE CLASS."

DEPLOYING CLASS ANALYSIS, TO BOOT!

"I DON'T BELIEVE IN THE **BILLIONAIRE AGENDA**, I DON'T BELIEVE IN THE **CORPORATE AGENDA**, AND I DON'T WANT THEIR MONEY.

THEY CAN HAVE ALL THE MONEY,

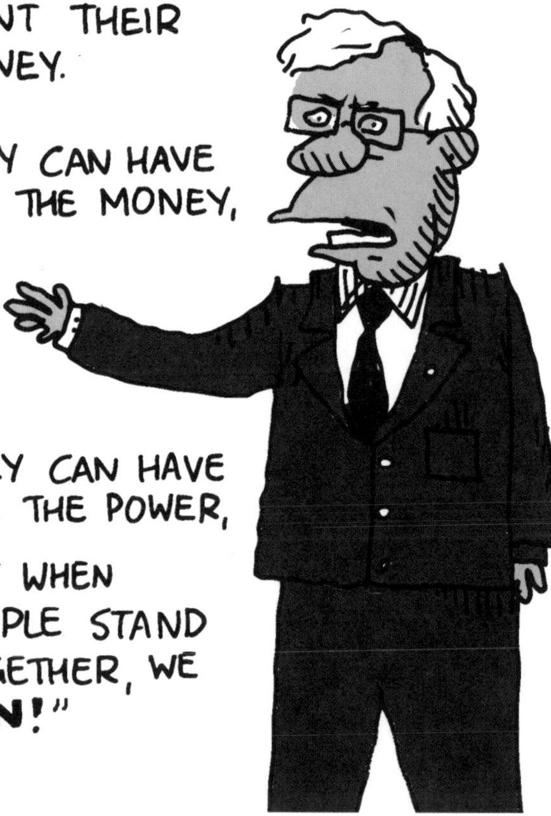

THEY CAN HAVE ALL THE POWER,

BUT WHEN PEOPLE STAND TOGETHER, WE **WIN!**"

THE MORE HE TALKED, THE HIGHER BERNIE'S POLLS ROSE.

COULD THE TRIANGULATION ERA BE OVER?

"WHEN WE BEGAN THIS CAMPAIGN ... THREE AND A HALF MONTHS AGO, A LOT OF THE MEDIA PUNDITS WERE SAYING, YEAH HE'S A NICE GUY, HE'S INTERESTING, BUT WHO REALLY IS GOING TO SUPPORT THE IDEA OF A POLITICAL REVOLUTION?"

"TURNS OUT, A WHOLE LOT OF PEOPLE."

THE DEMOCRATIC LEFT, LEFT IN THE COLD AND TAKEN FOR GRANTED FOR SO LONG, FINALLY HAD A VIABLE PRESIDENTIAL CANDIDATE -- ONE WILLING TO TALK ABOUT PROBLEMS AND SOLUTIONS THAT NEVER APPEARED IN MAINSTREAM POLITICAL DISCOURSE.

THERE IS **NO** RATIONAL REASON THAT 22% OF OUR KIDS ARE LIVING IN **POVERTY** OR WHY SENIORS HAVE TO GET BY ON $13,000 A YEAR. THAT'S **CRAP**. THAT'S UNACCEPTABLE.

YES!

BERNIE SANDERS

BERNIE UNDERSTOOD THE OUTSIZED ROLE OF BIG MONEY IN AMERICAN POLITICS. STILL, HE REFUSED THE LURE OF BIG CAMPAIGN CONTRIBUTIONS FROM MAJOR DONORS.

"IN THE SENATE, IN EVERY MEETING, THERE IS A DISCUSSION ABOUT HOW WE'RE DOING IN FUNDRAISING."

HE PREFERRED GRASSROOTS ORGANIZING.

"THERE HAS NOT BEEN ONE DISCUSSION ABOUT A POLITICAL RALLY. NOT ONE. NOT ONE THAT SAYS LET'S GO TO PHILADELPHIA AND BRING OUT 20,000 PEOPLE AND TALK ABOUT OUR AGENDA. NOT ONE. ALWAYS MONEY."

BERNIE'S CROWDS WERE HUGE AND GETTING BIGGER.

MEANWHILE, SUPPORT FOR THE "INEVITABLE" HILLARY CLINTON SEEMED MORE DUTIFUL THAN ENTHUSIASTIC.

THE SOCIALIST SENATOR FILLED STADIUMS. *POLITICO,* THE MAGAZINE FOR BELTWAY INSIDERS, CALLED IT "THE SUMMER OF SANDERS -- [A] STRING OF UNEXPECTEDLY LARGE CAMPAIGN RALLIES THAT'S EXCEEDING EVEN BARACK OBAMA'S 2007 DRAWS WITH ATTENDANCE THAT OFTEN NUMBERS IN THE TENS OF THOUSANDS."

WHAT HOWARD DEAN (NOW CO-OPTED INTO THE HILLARY CAMPAIGN) HAD ONCE CALLED "THE DEMOCRATIC WING OF THE DEMOCRATIC PARTY" HAD COME IN FROM THE COLD.

EVEN WITHOUT A BILLION-DOLLAR CAMPAIGN TO COORDINATE THEM, THEIR NUMBERS WERE TOO LARGE, AND THEY WERE TOO ENTHUSIASTIC, TO STILL BE DENIED A VOICE.

DLC-DOMINATED MILITANT CENTRISM WAS COMING TO AN END.

WITHIN THE FIRST TWO MONTHS OF THE CAMPAIGN, SURVEYS SHOWED BERNIE RAPIDLY CLOSING THE GAP IN THE IOWA CAUCUSES. HE LED IN THE NEW HAMPSHIRE PRIMARY. BUT THAT WASN'T ENOUGH TO WIN THE NOMINATION.

HE FACED AN UPHILL BATTLE, ESPECIALLY IN THE SOUTH. NEVERTHELESS, SOME PUNDITS BEGAN SAYING THE IMPOSSIBLE: THE SOCIALIST SENATOR MIGHT WIN.

THE SIGHT OF ANY DEMOCRAT RAISING BILLIONS WHILE OFFERING **VAGUE ASSURANCES OF FUTURE REFORM** WON'T SATISFY ANYONE AND COMES AT A HIGH OPPORTUNITY COST.

Ready for Hilly

Bill Curry, Salon

BERNIE HAD A LOT OF WORK TO DO. YOU CAN'T WIN THE NOMINATION WITHOUT STRONG SUPPORT FROM WOMEN AND BLACKS -- TWO DEMOGRAPHICS HILLARY WAS INHERITING FROM HER HUSBAND AND OBAMA. RATHER THAN BE DEFENSIVE, BERNIE ASSUMED A HUMBLE STANCE AFTER ACTIVISTS FROM BLACK LIVES MATTER, THE ORGANIZATION THAT FIGHTS POLICE BRUTALITY, BUM-RUSHED HIS CAMPAIGN APPEARANCES.

SOME ON THE ANTIWAR LEFT DISLIKED
SANDERS'S SUPPORT FOR ISRAEL. THEY
WERE DISAPPOINTED BY HIS TAMPED-DOWN
TONE OF DISMAY DURING ISRAEL'S BRUTAL
2014 INVASION AND BOMBING OF HAMAS-
CONTROLLED GAZA.

THIS IS A VERY DEPRESSING
AND DIFFICULT ISSUE. THIS
HAS GONE ON FOR 60
BLOODY YEARS.

LEFTIES WERE
DISGUSTED BY
THE DISPRO-
PORTIONATELY
HIGH DEATH
TOLL ON THE
PALESTINIAN
SIDE. THEY
WANTED BERNIE
TO SAY MORE.

HE'S IRKED BY THE CRITICISM.

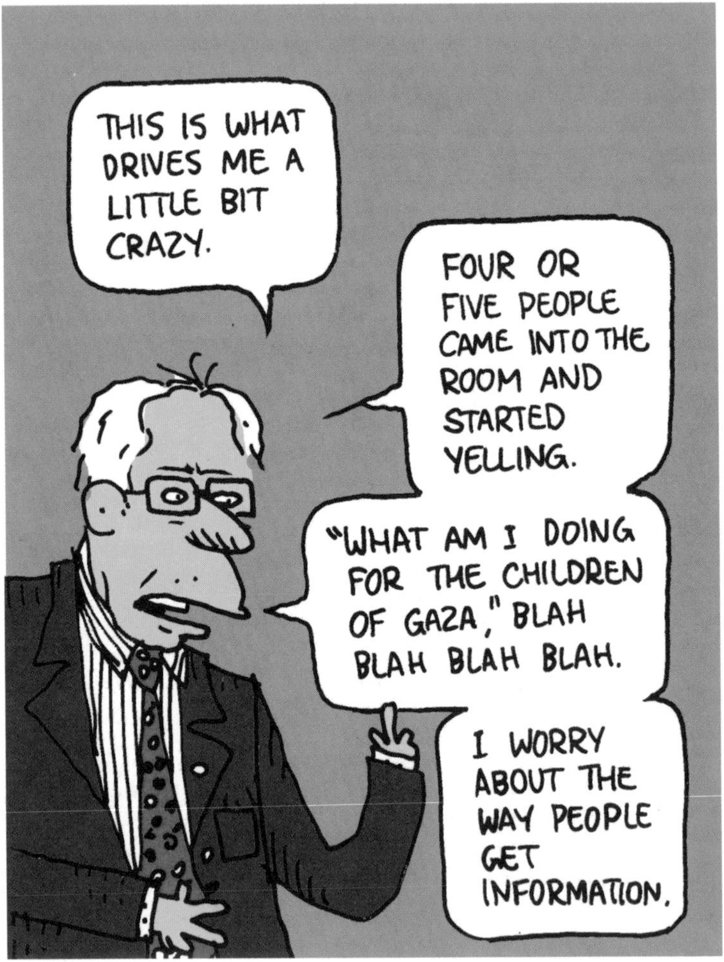

THIS IS WHAT DRIVES ME A LITTLE BIT CRAZY.
FOUR OR FIVE PEOPLE CAME INTO THE ROOM AND STARTED YELLING.
"WHAT AM I DOING FOR THE CHILDREN OF GAZA," BLAH BLAH BLAH BLAH.
I WORRY ABOUT THE WAY PEOPLE GET INFORMATION.

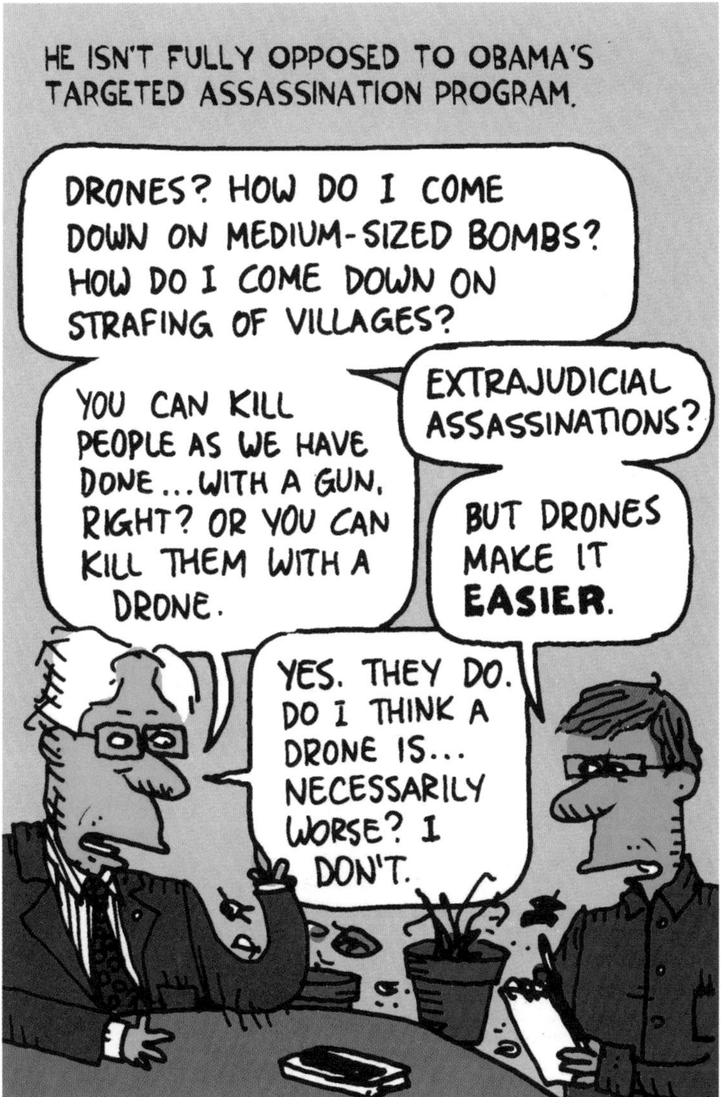
HE ISN'T FULLY OPPOSED TO OBAMA'S TARGETED ASSASSINATION PROGRAM.
DRONES? HOW DO I COME DOWN ON MEDIUM-SIZED BOMBS? HOW DO I COME DOWN ON STRAFING OF VILLAGES?
EXTRAJUDICIAL ASSASSINATIONS?
YOU CAN KILL PEOPLE AS WE HAVE DONE...WITH A GUN, RIGHT? OR YOU CAN KILL THEM WITH A DRONE.
BUT DRONES MAKE IT **EASIER**.
YES. THEY DO. DO I THINK A DRONE IS... NECESSARILY WORSE? I DON'T.

THEN THERE WAS THE GHOST OF 2000.
DEMOCRATS STILL FEARED A NADER-LIKE
CHALLENGER FROM THE LEFT WHO
BECOMES A "SPOILER" -- A CANDIDATE
WHO DIVIDES THE DEMOCRATIC VOTE AND
HANDS VICTORY TO THE REPUBLICANS.
THE ONLY WAY BERNIE SANDERS COULD
OVERCOME THAT WORRY WOULD BE TO
BECOME SO POPULAR, SO FAST, THAT
VOTERS AND PUNDITS BELIEVE THAT *HE'S*
THE INEVITABLE CANDIDATE AND THAT
HILLARY, IF SHE STAYED IN THE RACE,
WOULD BE THE REAL SPOILER.

TO WIN, BERNIE WOULD HAVE TO CREATE
THE IMPRESSION WITHIN THE MEDIA AND
MONEYED GATEKEEPERS WHO DECIDE
AMERICAN ELECTIONS THAT HE CAN WIN.

WOULD HE WIN? COULD HE? HIS DESIRE TO
FIGHT A CLEAN CAMPAIGN FORCED HIM TO
FIGHT A TOUGH OPPONENT WITH ONE
HAND TIED BEHIND HIS BACK.

THE AMERICAN PEOPLE ARE SICK AND TIRED OF HEARING ABOUT YOUR DAMN E-MAILS!!

In which Bernie neutralized Hillary's biggest vulnerability, her illegal use of a private server for State Department business.

THE ODDS WERE AGAINST HIM. BUT HE'D
BEATEN FORMIDABLE ODDS BEFORE. WHETHER
AS PRESIDENT, OR AS SENATOR, OR
PERHAPS AS A CABINET MEMBER, BERNIE WILL
REVOLUTIONIZE ELECTORAL POLITICS.
BECAUSE HE DOESN'T KNOW HOW TO DO
ANYTHING ELSE.

"GIVEN THE CRISES THAT WE FACE AT THIS PARTICULAR MOMENT— THE **ECONOMIC** CRISIS, THE **CLIMATE CHANGE** CRISIS, THE **CAMPAIGN FINANCE** CRISIS, THE **POVERTY CRISIS**— RIGHT NOW, IF WE'RE GOING TO ADDRESS THESE ISSUES, IT CANNOT BE DONE

WITH ESTABLISHMENT POLITICS AND ESTABLISHMENT ECONOMICS.

WE HAVE TO GO **BEYOND THAT.**"

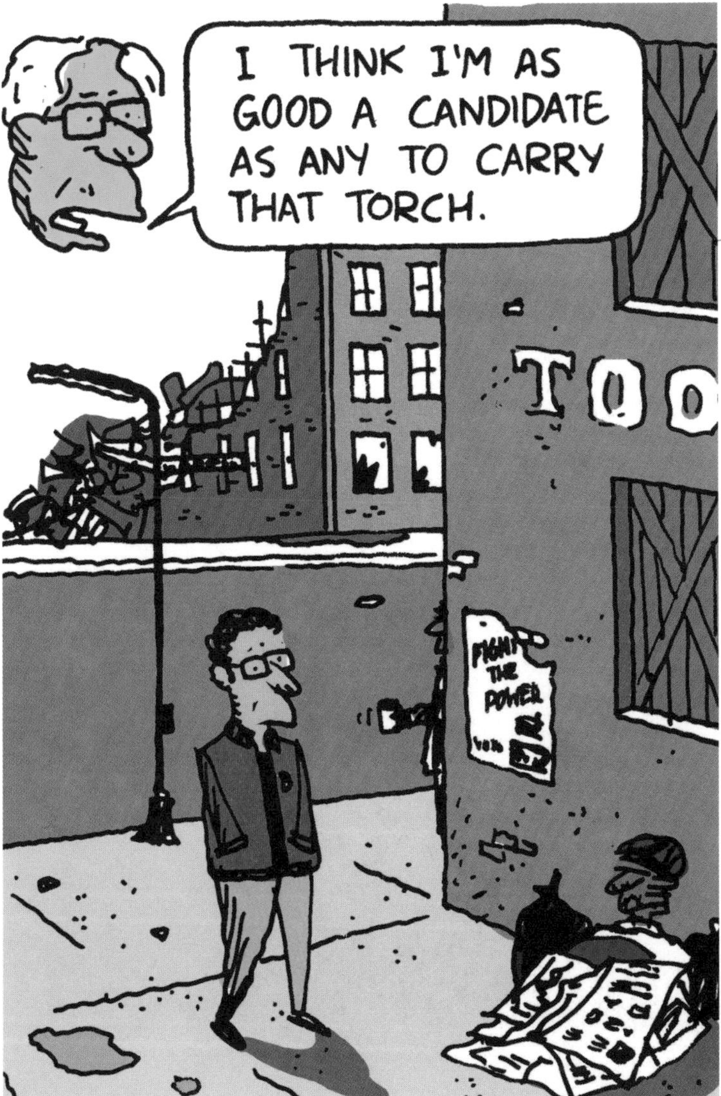
I THINK I'M AS GOOD A CANDIDATE AS ANY TO CARRY THAT TORCH.
TOO
FIGHT THE POWER

Afterword

After a person is radicalized, whether they're motivated by disgust at unfairness or a strong desire to fix a problem, they're presented with a choice between two roads: the way of the rebel and that of the reformer.

My first comics biography deals with the consummate rebel, Edward Snowden. To those in authority, there is no more worrisome (or loathsome) revolutionary than one of their own who turns against the system, betrays his oaths of fealty, and uses his inside knowledge in order to attack it. Snowden worked for the Central Intelligence Agency, the National Security Agency, and several private contracting firms, stole documents that showed that his employers were breaking the law on a massive scale, and turned them over to the news media so they could tell the truth to the world. It is no wonder that the United States government is so eager to get him back "home" and behind bars.

Bernie's political credibility, his currency with ordinary voters and Americans in general, derives from his willingness to tolerate years of ridicule and contempt for his self-description as a "democratic socialist," much of it from his colleagues in the Senate. Now that capitalism doesn't look so good, not in Greece and certainly not in Dayton, Ohio, the one guy out of 400-plus members of Congress to have been calling for a "political revolution" for decades is the only game in town for people who like their revolts served lukewarm, i.e., from inside the Beltway. Bernie Sanders is an outsider who tries to effect change from within the system.

There is no doubt that rebels like Snowden are heroes. Whatever you think of his morals, only a fool would doubt his courage.

It is tougher, in some ways, to try to effect change from the inside. Mainly this is because few still believe that it's possible.

It's a delicate balance, this sneaky end-run around revolution. Push too hard for what you and your supporters believe in, and you'll certainly be alienated and marginalized by the gatekeepers of the mainstream media. Fail to push hard enough and you won't get the job done.

The massive crowds that began coming to Bernie's campaign rallies after he announced his run for president, many of them drawn from the ranks of the young, demonstrate that there is a raging appetite for new leadership. If Bernie turns lame, or stays true and loses the nomination or the election, the hundreds of thousands of voters who turned out will never do so again. They will become jaded and cynical, much like the young men and women who canvassed for Obama in 2008, only to find out after the election that their politics bore little resemblance to his.

That, I suspect, is something that Bernie would hate to see. How he manages to avoid such a dismal outcome will be fascinating to watch.

TED RALL

Notes

7. "Transcript: Bernie Sanders's Remarks at the Iowa State Fair—Part 1," WhatTheFolly.com, August 17, 2015, http://www. whatthefolly.com/2015/08/17/transcript-bernie-sanderss-remarks-at-the-iowa-state-fair-part-1/.

8. "Transcript: Bernie Sanders's Remarks at the Iowa State Fair—Part 1," WhatTheFolly.com, August 17, 2015, http://www. whatthefolly.com/2015/08/17/transcript-bernie-sanderss-remarks-at-the-iowa-state-fair-part-1/.

9. "Transcript: Bernie Sanders's Remarks at the Iowa State Fair—Part 4," WhatTheFolly.com, August 17, 2015, http://www.whatthefolly. com/2015/08/17/transcript-bernie-sanderss-remarks-at-the-iowa-state-fair-part-4/.

10. Patrick Healy, "Hillary Clinton's Rivals Critical of Democratic Party Politics," New York Times, August 28, 2015, http://www.nytimes. com/2015/08/29/us/politics/bernie-sanders-faces-skepticism-from-democratic-insiders.html.

14. Thomas Eagleton, a former U.S. senator from Missouri, was the Democratic vice presidential nominee under George McGovern in 1972. When it was revealed that he had received medical treatments for depression, the McGovern campaign forced Eagleton to quit the race. Detractors viewed McGovern as having poor judgment for selecting him in the first place, and then as lacking courage after he dumped him as his running mate.

18. Jimmy Carter, Public Papers of the Presidents of the United States: Jimmy Carter, 1980–81. Washington, D.C.: Government Printing Office, 1981.

20. Bernie Sanders, interview by Ted Rall.

26. Jimmy Carter, *Public Papers of the Presidents of the United States: Jimmy Carter, 1980–81*. Washington, D.C.: Government Printing Office, 1981.

27. "Senator Edward M. Kennedy 'The Cause Endures,'" *History Place*, http://www.historyplace.com/speeches/tedkennedy.htm.

28. Gallup Presidential Polls 1936–2000," Atlas Forum, April 29, 2010, http://uselectionatlas.org/FORUM/index.php?topic=115543.0.
    Adam Clymer, "Democratic Rules Changes Produce Few Conflicts," *New York Times*, January 17, 1982, http://www.nytimes.com/1982/01/17/us/democratic-rules-changes-produce-few-conflicts.html.

30. Steven F. Hayward, "How Reagan Became Reagan," *Claremont Review of Books*, August 30, 2004, http://www.claremont.org/article/how-reagan-became-reagan.
    "The 1982 Recession," PBS.org, http://www.pbs.org/wgbh/americanexperience/features/general-article/reagan-recession/.

31. Arthur Herman, "Obama Can Learn Strength from Jimmy Carter," *New York Post*, March 13, 2014, http://nypost.com/2014/03/13/obama-can-learn-strength-from-jimmy-carter.
    Chart: "Total Military Spending," http://media.nj.com/njv_guest_blog/photo/total-us-military-spending-chartjpg-73d7131703c72e61.jpg.

32. Massimo Calabresi, "Remembering 1980: Are the Polls Missing Something?," *Time*, October 31, 2012, http://swampland.time.com/2012/10/31/remembering-1980-are-the-polls-missing-something.

36. William Schneider, "Dukakis, Gephardt Emerge in a Search for Surrogates," *Los Angeles Times*, May 31, 1987, http://articles.latimes.com/1987-05-31/opinion/op-9517_1_dukakis-administration/2.

39. Adam T. Thomas, "Sit This One Out, Ralph," *Harvard Crimson*, January 21, 2004, http://www.thecrimson.com/article/2004/1/21/sit-this-one-out-ralph-according/.

41. Adam Nagourney, "Centrist Democrats Warn Party Not to Present Itself as 'Far Left,'" *New York Times*, July 29, 2003, http://www.nytimes.com/2003/07/29/us/centrist-democrats-warn-party-not-to-present-itself-as-far-left.html.

42. William Schneider, "Feuding Democrats: It's the 'Me Too' Wing vs the 'We Told You So' Faction, *Los Angeles Times*, May 19, 1991, http://articles.latimes.com/1991-05-19/opinion/op-3030_1_democratic-party.

43. Margaret Weir, ed., *The Social Divide: Political Parties and the Future of Activist Government* (Washington, D.C.: Brookings Institution Press, 1998), 317.
   "Bill Clinton's Campaign Promises," TheForbiddenKnowledge.com, http://www.theforbiddenknowledge.com/hardtruth/bill_clinton_promises.htm.

44. It shouldn't be forgotten that Clinton won with 43 percent of the vote and might very well not have done so if Ross Perot had not drained off 19 percent.

48. "Clinton's Economic Plan: The Speech; Text of the President's Address to a Joint Session of Congress," *New York Times*, February 18, 1993, http://www.nytimes.com/1993/02/18/us/clinton-s-economic-plan-speech-text-president-s-address-joint-session-congress.html.

51. Zaid Jilani, "GRAPH: As Union Membership Has Declined, Income Inequality Has Skyrocketed in the United States," *ThinkProgress*, March 3, 2011, http://thinkprogress.org/politics/2011/03/03/147994/unions-income-inequality/.
   Brian J. McCabe, "Primary Voter Turnout Stays Low, but More So for Democrats," *FiveThirtyEight*, September 14, 2010, http://fivethirtyeight.blogs.nytimes.com/2010/09/14/primary-voter-turnout-stays-low-but-more-so-for-democrats.

55. Martin Kettle, "Florida 'Recounts' Make Gore Winner," *Guardian*, January 28, 2001, http://www.theguardian.com/world/2001/jan/29/uselections2000.usa.

"Gore Concedes Presidential Race After the Fight of His Life," *Guardian*, December 13, 2000, http://www.theguardian.com/world/2000/dec/14/uselections2000.usa12.

Peter Hartcher, "Taste the Difference," *Sydney Morning Herald*, November 23, 2007, http://www.smh.com.au/articles/2007/11/22/1195321949441.html?page=fullpage.

56. "No Sympathy for Spoiler Nader," *Orlando Sentinel*, February 5, 2001, http://articles.orlandosentinel.com/2001-02-05/news/0102050069_1_nader-green-party-conceit.

59. Frank Newport, "Socialism Viewed Positively by 36% of Americans," Gallup, February 4, 2010, http://www.gallup.com/poll/125645/socialism-viewed-positively-americans.aspx.

Robert B. Reich, *Locked in the Cabinet* (New York: Vintage, 1998).

60. Angie Drobnic Holan, "Obama Statements on Single-Payer Have Changed a Bit," *Politifact*, July 16, 2009, http://www.politifact.com/truth-o-meter/statements/2009/jul/16/barack-obama/obama-statements-single-payer-have-changed-a-bit/.

Angie Drobnic Holan, "Public Option Was in Obama's Platform," *Politifact*, December 23, 2009, http://www.politifact.com/truth-o-meter/statements/2009/dec/23/barack-obama/public-option-obama-platform/.

61. Julia La Roche, "REVEALED: More Details on the Fed's Breathtaking $7.7 Trillion in Loans to Large Banks," *Business Insider*, November 27, 2011, http://www.businessinsider.com/bank-bailouts-2011-11-27.

Martha M. Hamilton and Lukas Pleva, "Did the Stimulus Cost More than the War in Iraq?," *Politifact*, August 25, 2010, http://www.politifact.com/truth-o-meter/statements/2010/aug/25/mark-tapscott/did-stimulus-cost-more-war-iraq/.

Angie Drobnic Holan, "Obama has Praised Single-Payer Plans in the Past," *Politifact*, August 12, 2009, http://www.politifact.com/truth-o-meter/statements/2009/aug/12/barack-obama/obama-has-praised-single-payer-plans-past/.

Tami Luhby, "Obama Signs Jobless Benefit Extension," CNN, November 6, 2009, http://money.cnn.com/2009/11/05/news/economy/Extending_unemployment_benefits/.

62. John Bradford, "Inequality and Stratification," SlideShare, November 7, 2012, http://www.slideshare.net/jbradfo4/bradford-mvsu-fall-2012-intro-211-stratification-and-inequality.

63. Brad Plumer, "The U.S. Labor Force Is Still Shrinking. Here's Why," *Washington Post*, November 8, 2013, https://www.washingtonpost.com/news/wonk/wp/2013/11/08/the-u-s-labor-force-is-still-shrinking-rapidly-heres-why/.

64. Kayla Webley, "Why Can't You Discharge Student Loans in Bankruptcy?," *Time*, February 9, 2012, http://business.time.com/2012/02/09/why-cant-you-discharge-student-loans-in-bankruptcy/.

Jeffrey Sparshott, "Congratulations, Class of 2015. You're the Most Indebted Ever (For Now)," *Wall Street Journal*, May 8, 2015, http://blogs.wsj.com/economics/2015/05/08/congratulations-class-of-2015-youre-the-most-indebted-ever-for-now/.

65. Chalmers Johnson, "737 U.S. Military Bases=Global Empire," *AlterNet*, February 18, 2007, http://www.alternet.org/story/47998/737_u.s._military_bases_%3D_global_empire

71. Stephanie McMillan, *The Beginning of the American Fall: A Comics Journalist Inside the Occupy Wall Street Movement* (New York: Seven Stories Press, 2012).

Christopher Robbins, "Justice Dept: Homeland Security Advised Raids on Occupy Wall Street Camps," *Gothamist*, November 16, 2011, http://gothamist.com/2011/11/16/justice_dept_official_raids_of_occu.php.

Colleen Long and Verena Dobnik, "Zuccotti Park Eviction: Police Arrest 200 Wall Street Protesters," *Huffington Post*, January 14, 2012, http://www.huffingtonpost.com/2011/11/15/zuccotti-park-eviction-po_n_1094306.html.

75. Paul Harris, "Bernie Sanders: America's No1 Socialist Makes His Move into the Mainstream," *Guardian*, October 21, 2011, http://www.theguardian.com/world/2011/oct/21/bernie-sanders-socialist-vermont-interview.

76. "Sanders Files 'Saving American Democracy Amendment,'" press release, December 8, 2011, http://www.sanders.senate.gov/newsroom/press-releases/sanders-files-saving-american-democracy-amendment.

Zaid Jilani, "Bernie Sanders Introduces Bill to Lift the Payroll Tax Cap, Ensuring Full Social Security Funding for Nearly 75 Years," *ThinkProgress*, August 25, 2011, http://thinkprogress.org/economy/2011/08/25/304387/bernie-sanders-introduces-bill-to-lift-the-payroll-tax-cap-ensuring-full-social-security-funding-for-nearly-75-years/.

Zaid Jilani, "Bernie Sanders Says It Would Be a 'Good Idea' to Primary President Obama," *ThinkProgress*, July 22, 2011, http://thinkprogress.org/special/2011/07/22/277124/bernie-sanders-primary-obama/.

78. Bernie Sanders, "What Can We Learn from Denmark?," *Huffington Post*, May 26, 2013, http://www.huffingtonpost.com/rep-bernie-sanders/what-can-we-learn-from-de_b_3339736.html.

80. Sarah Mimms, "Bernie Sanders Is a Loud, Stubborn Socialist. Republicans Like Him Anyway," *National Journal*, July 27, 2015, http://www.nationaljournal.com/2016-elections/bernie-sanders-is-a-loud-stubborn-socialist-republicans-like-him-anyway-20150727.

81. Manu Raju and Burgess Everett, "Sanders' Senate Colleagues Stunned by His Ascent," *Politico*, July 13, 2015, http://www.politico.com/story/2015/07/bernie-sanders-2016-senate-colleagues-opinions-120007.html#ixzz3hDYCJkbv.

82. David Weigel, "Bernie Sanders's 27 Years of Israel Answers," *Washington Post*, August 4, 2015, http://www.washingtonpost.com/news/post-politics/wp/2015/08/04/bernie-sanderss-27-years-of-israel-answers/.

Matt Wilstein, "'Excuse Me! Shut Up!': Bernie Sanders Defends Israel from Town Hall Hecklers," *Mediaite*, August 20, 2014, http://www.mediaite.com/online/excuse-me-shut-up-bernie-sanders-defends-israel-from-town-hall-hecklers/.

83. "Domestic Weekly Update December 22, 2009," Results.org, http://www.results.org/take_action/domestic_weekly_update_december_22_2009/.

84. Burlington Free Press, "Snowden Deserves Leniency, Sanders Says," *USA Today*, January 6, 2014, http://www.usatoday.com/story/news/nation/2014/01/06/snowden-clemency-sanders-nsa/4344467/.

85. Lucy Madison, "Elizabeth Warren: 'There Is Nobody in This Country Who Got Rich on His Own," CBS News, September 22, 2011, http://www.cbsnews.com/news/elizabeth-warren-there-is-nobody-in-this-country-who-got-rich-on-his-own/.

86. Harris, "Bernie Sanders."

87. Harris, "Bernie Sanders."

88. "Socialism," *1896: The Presidential Campaign. Cartoons & Commentary*, http://projects.vassar.edu/1896/socialism.html.

89. "It Takes More Than That to Kill a Bull Moose: The Leader and the Cause," *Theodore Roosevelt Association*, http://www.theodoreroosevelt.org/site/c.elKSIdOWIiJ8H/b.9297449/k.861A/It_Takes_More_Than_That_to_Kill_a_Bull_Moose_The_Leader_and_The_Cause.htm.

90. "Huey P. Long," *American Rhetoric*, http://www.americanrhetoric.com/speeches/hueyplongshare.htm.

91. "Henry Wallace criticizes Truman's Cold War Policies," History.com, http://www.history.com/this-day-in-history/henry-wallace-criticizes-trumans-cold-war-policies.

92. Bernie Sanders, interview by Ted Rall.

93. Bernie Sanders, interview by Ted Rall.

95. Harris, "Bernie Sanders."

97. Bernie Sanders, interview by Ted Rall.

100. Bernie Sanders, interview by Ted Rall.

103. Conference Board of Canada, "Income Inequality, Mid-1990s and Late 2000s," http://www.conferenceboard.ca/Libraries/PUBLIC_IMAGES/worldInequality_chart2.sflb.

104. Mark Leibovich, "The Socialist Senator," New York Times, January 21, 2007, http://www.nytimes.com/2007/01/21/magazine/21Sanders.t.html.

105. Jason Horowitz, "Bernie Sanders's '100% Brooklyn' Roots Are as Unshakable as His Accent," New York Times, July 24, 2015, http://www.nytimes.com/2015/07/25/us/politics/bernie-sanderss-100-brooklyn-roots-show-beyond-his-accent.html.

106. Bernie Sanders, interview by Ted Rall.

107. Bernie Sanders, interview by Ted Rall.

108. Bernie Sanders, interview by Ted Rall.

109. Kurt F. Stone, The Jews of Capitol Hill: A Compendium of Jewish Congressional Members (Washington, D.C.: Scarecrow Press, 2010).

110. Bernie Sanders, interview by Ted Rall.

111. Bernie Sanders, interview by Ted Rall.

114. Bernie Sanders, interview by Ted Rall.

115. Bernie Sanders, interview by Ted Rall.

116. Bernie Sanders, interview by Ted Rall.

117. Horowitz, "Bernie Sanders's '100% Brooklyn' Roots."

118. Horowitz, "Bernie Sanders's '100% Brooklyn' Roots."
    Bernie Sanders, interview by Ted Rall.

119. Bernie Sanders, interview by Ted Rall.

120. Bernie Sanders, interview by Ted Rall.

121. Horowitz, "Bernie Sanders's '100% Brooklyn' Roots."

124. Leibovich, "The Socialist Senator."
    Bernie Sanders, interview by Ted Rall.

125. Bernie Sanders, interview by Ted Rall.

126. Rick Perlstein, "A Political Education," *University of Chicago Magazine*, Jan.–Feb. 2015, http://mag.uchicago.edu/law-policy-society/political-education.

127. Kurt F. Stone, *The Jews of Capitol Hill: A Compendium of Jewish Congressional Members* (Washington, D.C.: Scarecrow Press, 2010).

129. Naomi Zeveloff, "My Quixotic Hunt for Bernie Sanders' Kibbutz," *Forward*, September 3, 2015, http://forward.com/news/320344/my-quixotic-hunt-for-bernie-sanders-kibbutz/.
    Bernie Sanders, interview by Ted Rall.

132. Jess Wisslowski and Anne Galloway, "Bernie Sanders' Early Days in Vermont: His Life, Loves and Circuitous Route to Politics," VTDigger.org, July 9, 2015, http://vtdigger.org/2015/07/09/bernie-sanders-early-days-in-vermont-his-life-loves-and-circuitous-route-to-politics/.

137. "Welcome To The Liberty Union Party," Liberty Union Party, http://www.libertyunionparty.org/?page_id=8.

143. Bernie Sanders, interview by Ted Rall.

144. Bernie Sanders, interview by Ted Rall.

146. Mark Binelli, "Weekend with Bernie," *Rolling Stone*, July 9, 2015, http://www.rollingstone.com/politics/news/weekend-with-bernie-sanders-20150709?page=7.

148. Binelli, "Weekend with Bernie."

149. Paul Lewis, "Inside the Mind of Bernie Sanders: Unbowed, Unchanged, and Unafraid of a Good Fight," *Guardian*, June 19, 2015, http://www.theguardian.com/us-news/2015/jun/19/bernie-sanders-profile-democrat-presidential-candidate.

156. "Statement on Impeachment," press release, April 20, 2007, http://www.sanders.senate.gov/newsroom/press-releases/statement-on-impeachment.

157. "Bernie Not 'Democrat' Enough, Let's See How He Stacks Up," *Daily Kos*, August 31, 2015, http://www.dailykos.com/story/2015/08/31/1417001/-Bernie-Not-Democrat-Enough-Let-s-See-How-He-Stacks-Up#.

160. Nina Burleigh, "Bernie Sanders' War on the Banks," *Salon*, October 25, 2011, http://www.salon.com/2011/10/25/bernie_sanders_war_on_the_banks/.
"Sanders Votes No on Geithner: '[He's] More of a Part of the Problem . . . than the Solution," *Democracy Now*, January 29, 2009, http://www.democracynow.org/2009/1/28/sanders_votes_no_on_geithner_hes.

161. Harris, "Bernie Sanders."
Burleigh, "Sanders' War."

164. Harris, "Bernie Sanders."

167. Ron Kampeas, "Bernie Sanders, Lone Socialist in Congress, Pushes 'Jewish' Battle Against Inequality," *Forward*, January 14, 2014, http://forward.com/news/breaking-news/190913/bernie-sanders-lone-socialist-in-congress-pushes-j/#ixzz3hDu3XDqf.

169. Bernie Sanders, interview by Ted Rall.

170. Dan Merica, "Bernie Sanders Is Running for President," CNN, April 30, 2015, http://www.cnn.com/2015/04/29/politics/bernie-sanders-announces-presidential-run/.

171. Bernie Sanders, interview by Ted Rall.

172. Seth A. Richardson and Ray Hagar, "Bernie Sanders Rally Draws Crowds of 4,500 in Reno," Reno Gazette-Journal, August 19, 2015, http://www.rgj.com/story/news/politics/2015/08/19/bernie-sanders-rally-draws-crowd/31967175/.
    Jacqueline Policastro, "Political Revolution? Bernie Sanders Supporters Rally in Reno," KOLOTV.com, August 19, 2015, http://www.kolotv.com/home/headlines/Bernie_Sanders_Rally_UNR-322239262.html.

173. Seth A. Richardson and Ray Hagar , "Bernie Sanders rally draws crowd of 4,500 in Reno," Reno Press-Gazette, August 19, 2015, http://www.rgj.com/story/news/politics/2015/08/19/bernie-sanders-rally-draws-crowd/31967175/
    Isabella Castillo, "Bernie Sanders Speaks About Income Inequality to His Largest Audience Yet at Phoenix Rally," State Press, July 18, 2015, http://www.statepress.com/article/2015/07/bernie-sanders-speech.
    Richardson and Hagar, "Bernie Sanders Rally."
    Terri Hendry, "Bernie Sanders Gives Passionate Speech to Reno Supporters," MyNews4.com, August 18, 2015, http://www.mynews4.com/mostpopular/story/Bernie-Sanders-in-Reno/V168fs78s06dV4PXSJHs1A.cspx.

174. "Bernie Sanders tells 4,000 at University of Nevada crowd his 'revolution' has momentum," Nevada Appeal, August 19, 2015, http://www.nevadaappeal.com/news/17782758-113/bernie-sanders-tells-4000-at-university-of-nevada.

175. Bernie Sanders, interview by Ted Rall.

176. Bernie Sanders, interview by Ted Rall.

177. Ben Schrekinger, "How Bernie Sanders Makes His Mega-Rallies," *Politico*, August 19, 2015, http://www.politico.com/story/2015/08/bernie-sanders-rallies-2016-grassroots-support-121512.html.

179. Ben Wolfgang, "Bernie Sanders Surges in Iowa, New Hampshire as 'Fiery Authenticity' Resonates," *Washington Times*, August 16, 2015, http://www.washingtontimes.com/news/2015/aug/16/bernie-sanders-popularity-surges-in-iowa-new-hamps/.
    Bernie Sanders, interview by Ted Rall.

180. Bernie Sanders, interview by Ted Rall.

181. Bill Curry, "Here's How Bernie Sanders Could Win: the One Issue Where Hillary's Vulnerable, and Where the Tea Party Might Be Right," *Salon*, June 14, 2015, http://www.salon.com/2015/06/14/heres_how_bernie_sanders_could_win_the_one_issue_where_hillarys_vulnerable_and_where_the_tea_party_might_be_right/.
    Josh Nathan-Kazis, "Is Bernie Sanders a Lefty on Everything Except for Israel?," *Forward*, June 16, 2015, http://forward.com/news/national/310087/is-bernie-sanders-a-lefty-except-for-israel/.

182. Bernie Sanders, interview by Ted Rall.

183. Bernie Sanders, interview by Ted Rall.

185. Ben Jacobs and Sabrina Siddiqui, "Bernie Sanders to Clinton: People 'Are Sick of Hearing About Your Damn Emails,'" *Guardian*, October 13, 2015, http://www.theguardian.com/us-news/2015/oct/13/bernie-sanders-hillary-clinton-damn-email-server.

186. Bernie Sanders, interview by Ted Rall.

187. Bernie Sanders, interview by Ted Rall.

About the Author

Twice the winner of the Robert F. Kennedy Journalism Award and a Pulitzer Prize finalist, TED RALL is a syndicated political cartoonist, opinion columnist, graphic novelist, and occasional war correspondent whose work has appeared in hundreds of publications, including the *New York Times*, *Washington Post*, *Village Voice*, and *Los Angeles Times*. For Seven Stories Press he is the illustrator of the full-length comic *Billionaires & Ballot Bandits: How to Steal an Election in 9 Easy Steps* (2012), written by Greg Palast, and the author and illustrator of *The Book of Obama* (2012) and *The Anti-American Manifesto* (2010). His most recent books are *After We Kill You, We Will Welcome You Back as Honored Guests* (Hill and Wang, 2014) and *Snowden* (Seven Stories Press, 2015).